# Transforming the Next Generation of Leaders

# Transforming the Next Generation of Leaders

*Developing Future Leaders for a Disruptive, Digital-Driven Era of the Fourth Industrial Revolution (Industry 4.0)*

Sattar Bawany

**BEP** BUSINESS EXPERT PRESS

First published in 2019 by
Business Expert Press, LLC
222 East 46th Street, New York, NY 10017
www.businessexpertpress.com

ISBN-13: 978-1-94944-304-2 (paperback)
ISBN-13: 978-1-94944-305-9 (e-book)

Business Expert Press Human Resource Management and Organizational Behavior Collection

Collection ISSN: 1946-5637 (print)
Collection ISSN: 1946-5645 (electronic)

Cover and interior design by S4Carlisle Publishing Services Private Ltd., Chennai, India

First edition: 2019

10 9 8 7 6 5 4 3 2 1

Printed in the United States of America.

# Praise for Transforming the Next Generation of Leaders

"Today, business takes place in a highly disruptive and digital-driven landscape resulting in the need for companies to deliver its 'next generation' of leaders who are capable of leading now. This is a highly recommended book where Sattar has offered a pragmatic, tested, and insightful approaches including executive and transition coaching to effectively develop a sustainable leadership pipeline."

—Dr. Marshall Goldsmith, #1 New York Times bestselling author of *Triggers, MOJO and What Got You Here Won't Get You There*; Thinkers 50 – #1 Executive Coach and the only two-time #1 Leadership Thinker in the World

"Sattar Bawany, one of the world's top coaches and leadership authorities, has created a powerful manifesto on the pillars of accelerating the development of future leaders. This book will transform how organizations both identify and develop high potentials and emerging leaders so they can continue to compete effectively in the VUCA world. In addition, organizations that embrace Sattar's sound advice will meet one of their most important responsibilities—which is helping talented future leaders become the best leaders and people they can be all in support of bringing greater abundance to the world. *Transforming the Next Generation of Leaders* is an absolute must-read for HR leaders, executives, and government leaders all over the world."

—John Mattone, #1 Authority on Intelligent Leadership & the World's Top Executive Coach

"Developing future or next generation of leaders continues to be one of the perennial and biggest challenges facing organizations today especially in view of the dramatically changing digital and highly disruptive business landscape. The book *Transforming the Next Generation of Leaders* identify the leadership competencies that are critical in today's business environment that is fast-paced, highly disruptive, and VUCA-driven and also provides business leaders with best practice approaches, framework, and tools that can be leveraged upon toward developing the next generation of leaders (high potentials). This is a recommended read for leaders at all levels across all industries."

—Prof. Howard Yu, Author of *LEAP: How to Thrive in a World Where Everything Can Be Copied* (2018) and LEGO Professor of Management and Innovation, IMD Business School

"*Transforming the Next Generation of Leaders* is a very timely and highly practical book that provides tips, tools, and resources that will help the organization to develop its leadership bench strength. Sattar pulls together his extensive executive and leadership development experience into a concise, engaging, and extremely helpful how-to format that helps you identify, assess, select, and develop high-potential talent as well as define key leadership competencies that are required for success in today's digital-driven era of the Fourth Industrial Revolution. A must-read for human resource and business professionals seeking to ensure their organization remains relevant in this new normal business environment."
—Rajeev Peshawaria, CEO of the Iclif Leadership and Governance Centre, Author of the Wall Street Journal and Amazon Bestseller *Open Source Leadership* (2017) and *Too Many Bosses, Too Few Leaders* (2011)

"The publication of *Transforming the Next Generation of Leaders: Developing Future Leaders for a Disruptive, Digital-Driven Era of the Fourth Industrial Revolution (Industry 4.0)* is very timely. At a time when everyone is talking about what the future and future talent and leaders would look like, and when the traditional ways to prepare our future leaders are being reviewed, Sattar gives a pragmatic solution and insights on how it can be done. Its practicality, ease of understanding, and use of common terms make it easy for users to implement them. It's not just a book; it's a guide for implementation."
—Sylvano Damanik, Vice Chairman, Korn Ferry Indonesia

"Ready to Be a NextGen Leader? The author, Prof. Bawany distilling his extensive knowledge and wealth of experience in developing future leaders at all levels into various frameworks and models that can be easily explained and replicated. The book will also provide you specific guidance and invaluable insights on how to develop a leadership pipeline for your organization. He has written a must-read primer for all business and functional leaders (not only HR) who wish to transform their high potentials and ensure success in this new era of Industry 4.0. Read this book and learn from one of the best thought leaders in the field of leadership and organizational development."
—Dato' Hj Mohd Redza Shah Abdul Wahid, CEO and Executive Director, Bank Muamalat Malaysia Berhad

"Industry 4.0 is a historic paradigm shift, yet bold digital transformation is being challenged by familiar roadblocks including a lack of leadership. Leadership 4.0 is about leaders creating their own digital transformation strategy and ensuring that it is aligned with the business and growth plans of their organizations. In his book, *Transforming the Next Generation of Leaders,*

Prof. Bawany has clearly articulated the key to organizational success in this new era of Fourth Industrial Revolution is that there must be a commitment to and sense of ownership on the part of the various stakeholders, including the boards of directors and senior leadership. This book is highly recommended for business leaders to develop their leadership pipeline and also for those willing to embrace this new world as it presents huge opportunities to be leveraged, offering the prospect of new markets and new customers."
—Farid Basir, Chief Human Capital Officer (CHCO), Telekom Malaysia

"Leaders will find this book valuable. It offers clear and practical advice on how to develop talent in their organizations in this time of disruption and change. It also provides valuable insights for those aspiring to future leadership roles on the steps they can take to develop their own leadership capabilities."
—Prof. Linley Lord, Pro-Vice Chancellor and President, Curtin Singapore Campus

"Sattar Bawany's message on the critical skills required for the next generation leaders is a great testament to the need for a renewed type of leadership in a highly disruptive, increasingly volatile, uncertain, complex, and ambiguous (VUCA) environment. A gem of a book on leading teams in the digital era."
—Ted TAN, Deputy Chief Executive Officer, Enterprise Singapore

"An excellent book by Prof. Sattar Bawany. It lays out leading-edge practice in developing leadership talent. Put into the context of 4 IR and the VUCA environment, it is a compelling read for senior management of companies."
—YM Ungku Harun Al'Rashid Bin Ahmad, Vice President, Group Human Capital & Administration, Johor Corporation Group

"This is a unique book, which skilfully addresses future leadership needs in a VUCA world, driven by digital innovation and Industry 4.0 in an intensified 'global war for talent.' The highly experienced skills of the author as an executive coach and a scholarly practitioner brilliantly addresses the question 'How do organizations develop the next generation of leaders to meet these challenges?' If you want to find out what the future holds for leaders and learn more about Industry 4.0 and VUCA, I highly recommend this book."
—Milé Terziovski, Professor of Entrepreneurship and Innovation and Department Chair, Business Technology and Entrepreneurship, Swinburne University of Technology

"Talent management for developing future leaders who have the capabilities and commitment needed for current and future organizational success become one of the biggest challenges that we are facing at Generali. Indeed this book has helped me and hopefully will help you also to explore the strategies in developing leaders in the era of VUCA-driven Fourth Industrial Revolution. Thanks to Prof. Sattar Bawany as well who spend his valuable time with me on developing my leadership team."
—Edy Tuhirman, CEO, PT Asuransi Jiwa Generali Indonesia

"This is a work where the author has cut through the very complex subject of leadership with a very structured and logical approach that makes very meaningful sense of this complexity. The work explores thoroughly the dynamism of current leadership thinking. It also provides a very insightful and practical perspective that any practicing manager must further explore within themselves to enable them to improve their performance as a leader. Highly recommended."
—Michael Wooi, CEO, International Professional Managers Association (IPMA)

"One of the key attributes of a good leader is to acknowledge the need for leadership transformation. It is unavoidable and must be confronted as it is this adoption that would keep any small or big organization vibrant and most importantly relevant.

Prof. Sattar's book offers you that indispensable insight, which is refreshing, thought-provoking, and relentlessly logical.

This magnificent contribution is most suited for business leaders who believe that changes are inevitable and are ready to transform."
—Dr. T. Chandroo, Chairman/CEO, Modern Montessori International Group Pte Ltd

"Though leaders and their organizations have been encountering VUCA conditions for at least the past decade, will they really be ready to contend with new disruption brought about by the 4th industrial revolution? *Transforming the Next Generation of Leaders* answers this question, and lays out a plan for how leaders, teams, and organizations can thrive in the new world."
—Brian O. Underhill, Founder and CEO, CoachSource, LLC.

"As we face the disruptive digital era of IR4.0, the next generation of leaders will find most of what they have learned in the past to be obsolete. To be successful, we need to constantly learn, unlearn, and relearn, and be nimble and adaptable.

This book is a must read for someone who holds a leadership position regardless of the industry. It includes best practices and contemporary approaches to leadership development and will be useful to any leader who wants to navigate the fast-paced disruptive digital landscape."

—Suhaimi Salleh, Founder and CEO, SSA Group

"One of the biggest challenges facing organizations today is that they are under greater pressure to develop future or next-generation leaders faster in response to the challenges of the highly disruptive and digital-driven era of the Fourth Industrial Revolution. This book is highly recommended as it targeted in scope and application and focuses on approaches that provide an understanding of the best practices and contemporary approaches to the identification, assessment, selection, and development of future leaders."

—Professor Noor Azizi Ismail, Vice Chancellor, Universiti Malaysia Kelantan

"I congratulate Sattar on the launch of this book. He has drawn on his wealth of knowledge and experience in human resource development and consulting to author this easy-to-read guide and reference for leaders and managers in this disruptive, digitalized, and transformative global operating environment."

—Patrick Tay, MP for West Coast GRC and Asst. Secretary-General, National Trade Union Congress (NTUC)

"We live in a business world that is evolving at a rapid pace. Companies have to act now to prepare their next wave of leaders to grow and succeed. Sattar brings to the forefront the talent management challenges at hand and what companies should be doing now to understand the competencies needed in our future leaders and prepare their organizations. This book is a simple and easy read, which provides a powerful roadmap and tools to help identify, assess, select, and develop future leaders."

—Dhirendra Shantilal, Global Board Director, Fircroft

"The book is a compendious read for leaders who aspire to bring their organization to the next tier in identifying and inculcating talent. It provides clear insight into the process of talent development and how to develop the next generation of leaders. An indispensable source of reference for all managers."

—Janet Quek, Regional L&D Director, South Asia, Aon Service Corporation—Human Resources

"Professor Sattar has been one of high intellect, always challenging the norm, and his provocative thoughts have always amazed me. I have enjoyed every interaction with him as he makes me reflect and think beyond . . . this is the epitome of a thought leader who is always raising the bar!"

—Nadiah Tan Abdullah, Chief Human Resources Officer, S P Setia

"I have known Prof. Sattar to be a visionary educator and practitioner who is passionate and convicted of how we as leaders should prepare ourselves to succeed in a VUCA world! His ability to put fact-based evidence to support his understanding of *Transforming the Next Generation of Leaders* is convincing. But more so than that is his practical approach to how this can and should be done. I strongly recommend this reading and, if possible, his interaction and engagement, should this important subject resonate strongly with you."

—Collin Chiew, Director of Corporate Solutions Agency, AIA Group

"It is my pleasure to highly recommend this book by Prof. Bawany who has a deep passion for helping individuals and organizations achieve maximum performance success and greatness. Drawing on his extensive background in leadership and coaching experience, Prof. Bawany lays out a very comprehensive view on how everyone who wants to build the NextGen leadership pipeline need to consider the critical ingredients for effectiveness, change, and success."

—Carmen Wee, Group CHRO, Surbana Jurong

"Rendering leadership to get results in today's context is no longer adequate. The next-generation leaders must also be well honed in leading transformation. I encourage readers to read this book to internalize the concept of transforming the next generation of leaders as it has the potential to make you a truly great leader."

—Dr. Ahmad Magad, JP, Secretary-General, Singapore Manufacturing Federation (SMF)

"I am personally very grateful to have known Prof. Sattar Bawany. I always enjoy our dialogue about talent and leadership development whenever he visits our Jakarta office during his executive coaching sessions. Our organization has benefited tremendously from his coaching support where he has transformed several of our executives by looking deeper into ourselves and increasing our self-awareness and self-control, and thus we could improve our leadership skills effectively. I believe this book would give lots of insights to the readers that effective leadership is the result of the continuous adjustment, adaptation, and right planning and execution."

—Rosalina Hanis, Human Resources Director, AstraZeneca Indonesia

"A whopper of a resource manual for any aspiring leader seeking a quick reference guide to help him or her navigate the challenges of leading in the digital age. It provides the reader with a comprehensive framework for developing the most relevant leadership competencies critical for professional success today and for the future."

—John Augustine Ong, Vice President, Human Resources—
Singapore Exchange

"This is one of the kinds of book that anticipates the need of the future leadership. Very contextual and future-proof idea!"

—Steven Augustino Yudiyantho, Senior VP Human Capital, Bank Mandiri, Indonesia

"Sattar Bawany is a forward-thinking executive development consultant, practitioner, and master executive coach. I am glad that he has finally put his experiences into a must-read book for anyone wanting to build a sustainable talent pipeline . . . Read this book and learn from one of the best."

—Cynthia Ooi, CHRO, Texchem Group, Malaysia

"A good read, with useful tips."

—Dr. Bernard Lim, Director of Leadership and Organisational Development, MOH Holdings Pte Ltd

"Developing the next generation of leaders to create value, inspire, and see around corners takes a new mindset. Sattar distills his wisdom from teaching next-generation leaders over the years into actionable insights for companies aiming to set themselves up well for the future of work."

—Diana Wu David, Author, *Future Proof: Reinventing Work in the Age of Acceleration*

# Dedication

*The experience of writing a book is both internally challenging and rewarding. None of this would have been possible without the following individuals:*

*To my late parents, for always loving and supporting me.*

*To my wife, Nora, for her inspiration and encouragement, without whose never-failing empathy, understanding, and patience, this book would not have been finished in half the time.*

*To my twin boys, Adam and Danial, who hopefully will be inspired to be the next generation of leaders who will make a difference in the lives of others.*

*To all the individuals I have had the opportunity to lead, be led by, or watch their leadership from afar including Wan Hussin Zoohri, Sin Boon Ann, Dan M. Khanna, Michael Wooi, Bonnie Hagemann, Ruby Ng-Chen and Rodney P. Watson.*

*Finally, I want to thank the Almighty most of all, because without Him I wouldn't be able to do any of this.*

# Abstract

A company's leadership pipeline is expected to deliver its "next generation" of leaders who are capable of leading now. It is evident that conventional leadership development practices are no longer adequate. Organizations need to incorporate the next-generation leadership competencies globally in order to address the development needs of their rising leaders.

The current digital transformation that underpins the Fourth Industrial Revolution (also known as Industry 4.0) has ushered in a new business environment that is fast, open, and responsive, resulting in a number of organizational and leadership challenges.

How do organizations develop the next generation of leaders to meet these challenges? This book is designed to provide insights into an understanding of the best practices and contemporary approaches to the identification, assessment, selection, and development of future leaders of an organization with a focus on executive and transition coaching as a development tool.

# Keywords

VUCA; Fourth Industrial Revolution; Industry 4.0; digitalization; cognitive readiness; emotional and social intelligence; next generation leaders; NextGen leadership; high potentials; leadership competencies; leadership pipeline; leading for the future

# Contents

# List of Figures

# List of Tables

# Preface

Today's businesses face unprecedented challenges operating in a global environment that is increasingly volatile, uncertain, complex, and ambiguous (VUCA). The explosion of data and unprecedented advances in computer processing power globally have dramatically increased the capacity to support decision making within various functional operations in organizations across industries. The world has moved well beyond basic and enhanced process automation and is entering into an era of cognitive automation leveraging on artificial intelligence and robotics. The World Economic Forum is calling this the "Fourth Industrial Revolution."

The impact of advanced technologies touches virtually every industry and organization on many levels, from strategic planning and marketing to supply chain management and customer service. Today, many individuals and organizations across the globe are exploiting this change to disrupt every industry. Uber, Alibaba, Airbnb, Netflix, and Tesla are just a few famous examples of companies that have transformed lifestyles, including the way people travel, shop, and stay, and there are many more.

Leaders in organizations are also confronted with increased competition, globalization, demand for growing social responsibilities, and a stream of technological revolutions causing disruption in the marketplace. Hence, leaders need to challenge their mental models in their efforts to build and sustain a high-performance organization. Effective leadership is the process of impacting and influencing people to achieve the desired results and prepare for the future. Leading in today's highly disruptive and increasingly VUCA-driven world is becoming much more challenging. There is no easy path to becoming a highly effective leader, and the challenge of being one seems almost insurmountable.

One of the biggest challenges facing organizations today is that they are facing greater pressure to develop future or next generation of leaders faster, in response to the dramatically changing digital and highly disruptive business landscape. Who are the next generation of leaders? What makes them great? What do business and HR leaders need to know about developing the next generation of leaders? What are the competencies and best practices tools that can be leveraged upon to lead successfully in today's fast-paced, highly disruptive, and VUCA-driven business environment?

Talent management represents an organization's efforts to attract, develop, and retain skilled and valuable employees. The goal is to have people with the capabilities and commitment needed for current and future organizational success. This includes the high potentials who are the "NextGen" or future leaders. An organization's talent pool, particularly its high-potential managerial talent, is often referred to as the leadership pipeline. A leadership pipeline is expected to deliver the "next generation" of leaders. The payoff is a supply of leadership talent that simultaneously achieves targets, strengthens and protects ethical reputation, and navigates transformational change in pursuit of a bright, competitive future.

In a highly disruptive, digital, and VUCA-driven era of the Fourth Industrial Revolution (also known as Industry 4.0), these upcoming leaders need to have a broader skillset, one that equips them to think and act globally. It is evident that conventional leadership development practices are no longer adequate. Organizations globally need to incorporate the next-generation leadership competencies in order to address the development needs of their upcoming leaders.

What is the role of leaders in transforming the organization to succeed in the digital world? How do organizations develop the next generation of leaders?

This book seeks to guide leaders to succeed in the highly disruptive, digital, and increasingly VUCA-driven era of the Fourth Industrial Revolution (Industry 4.0), by:

1. providing insights into the role of leaders in transforming the organization to succeed in the digital world;
2. understanding the best practices and contemporary approaches to developing the next generation of leaders;
3. developing and implementing appropriate programs to lead and engage their people to achieve desired results.

# CHAPTER 1

# The New Realities
# of Leadership

## Disruptive Innovation

Disruption has and will continue to fundamentally change the way we live and work. Today's society, including businesses, government, and individuals, is responding to the shifts that would have seemed unimaginable or unthinkable even a few years ago. Artificial intelligence (AI), robotics, Internet-of-Things (IoT), blockchain technology, and cloud computing are reinventing the workforce and will continue to impact the workplace for many years to come (Bawany 2018a). Drones and driverless cars are transforming supply chains and logistics, resulting in enhanced quality of life. The changing consumer behavior, including the preferences and expectations, in particular, of those of the millennials (better known as Gen Y) and of "digital natives" (also known as Gen Z, those born between 1995 and 2010) who have grown up in a completely digital world, has altered the consumption patterns and demand in every area of life, including transportation, travel, accommodation, education, and lifestyle (Bawany and Bawany 2015).

The way we live and work is about to go through a profound change. In some countries, this has already been happening for quite some time now. Rapid advances in many technologies are expected to continue disrupting many of the industries in the various economies, and the impact will be felt across the globe. Yet, research by the Centre for Executive Education (CEE) and Executive Development Associates (EDA) validated by other consulting and research organizations has found that the majority of businesses and their leaders aren't prepared for the coming age of disruption—and sadly we believe many of the unprepared won't survive in this highly disruptive, intensely volatile, uncertain, complex, and ambiguous world.

Technology has long been acknowledged as a disruptive force that has radically changed the nature of work, business, and society in general. In the 19th century, the Industrial Revolution altered the world and how business was being managed profoundly and permanently. Then came electrification, the automobile, and mass production, just to name a few massive technological changes that have reshaped the 20th century. In the 21st century, powerful digital technologies and the rise of Internet connectivity have created a knowledge-driven economy that has revolutionized the world to a larger extent and made a great impact and profound changes in human history toward the way we work, live, and do business every day.

We are witnessing a vast range of ever-advancing technologies that are driving disruptive innovations that will continue to change and redefine our world. Advanced technologies can simply be defined as emerging technologies that may enable new ways of doing business that result in an improved employee productivity and enhanced sustainability of the organization in the longer term. Disruptive innovation,[1] a term coined by Harvard Business School (HBS) Professor Clayton Christensen, can be described as "a process by which a product or service takes root initially in simple applications at the bottom of a market and then relentlessly moves up market, eventually displacing established competitors" (Christensen 1997).

The root causes of these transformative trends that are driving this current wave of disruption include technological growth, globalization,

---

[1]Given how extensively the phrase "disruptive innovation" has been invoked in the past 20 years, Christensen revisits that most famous of innovative ideas in the article, "What Is Disruptive Innovation?" published in the December 2015 issue of the *Harvard Business Review*. He asserts that the concept of disruptive innovation has proven to be a powerful way of thinking about innovation-driven growth. "Many leaders of small, entrepreneurial companies praise it as their guiding star; so do many executives at large, well-established organizations, including Intel, Southern New Hampshire University, and Salesforce. com" (Christensen 2015). Regrettably, Christensen believes that the disruption theory is in danger of becoming a victim of its own success. Despite broad dissemination, the theory's core concepts have been widely misunderstood and its basic tenets frequently misapplied. Furthermore, essential refinements in the theory over the past 20 years appear to have been overshadowed by the popularity of the initial formulation.

and demographic changes. We need to understand how the interaction between these forces has defined the present and will continue to shape the future by their impact on businesses, economies, industries, societies, and individual lives (Bawany 2018a).

## Demystifying VUCA: What It Means and Why It Matters

Today, we have to acknowledge that no matter where we live, work, or manage our businesses, there are lots of uncertainties around us, and these could be a result of political, economic, societal, and cultural changes. Across many industries, a rising tide of volatility, uncertainty, and business complexity is roiling markets and changing the nature of competition (Doheny, Nagali, and Weig 2012).

VUCA is an acronym that emerged from the U.S. Army (Whiteman 1998). They described the environment as a VUCA world, meaning that it was volatile, uncertain, complex, and ambiguous (see Figure 1.1). It describes the "fog of war"—the chaotic conditions that are encountered on a modern battlefield. Its relevance to leaders in business is clear, as these conditions are highly descriptive of the environment in which business is conducted every day.

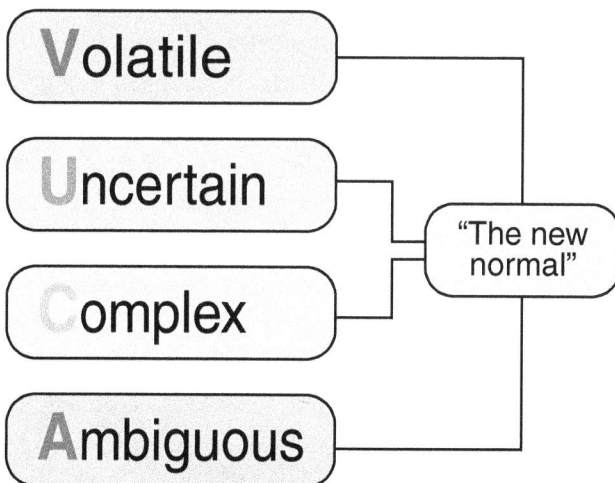

*Figure 1.1 The four elements of the VUCA business environment*

It is a challenging and rapidly changing and evolving business environment where not all the facts or interrelationships can possibly be known or identified. Leaders will often have to operate or make decisions without having all the facts or fully understanding the forces that may be influencing a situation or a business problem. Hence, there is a need for leaders to develop and demonstrate relevant skills and competencies so as to operate in this "new normal" and embrace this ambiguity and lead their organization to success with the right strategy and vision despite the chaotic environment in which they operate (Bawany 2018a).

However, leadership-as-usual, including creating a vision, is not enough in a VUCA world. Leaders need to understand the following implications of the characteristics of VUCA for their organization. Their relevance to today's workplace is clear, as these conditions are highly descriptive of the environment in which business is conducted today:

1. **Volatile:** Things change unpredictably, suddenly, and extremely, especially for the worse. There is a brutal increase in the four dimensions of changes we face today—type, speed, volume, and impact. An example would be a relatively unstable change where it is unexpected and may be of unknown duration. It is not necessarily hard to understand; knowledge about it is often available as in the case of prices of a raw material fluctuating after a natural disaster, such as when a fire takes out a supplier.

   Challenges faced are unexpected and mostly of unknown duration. We can overcome this challenge by gaining knowledge and being well prepared with the information and resources necessary.

2. **Uncertain:** As a result of volatility, we are unable to predict future events, resulting in lack of knowledge of important information; being doubtful and unclear about the present situation and future outcomes; and not being able to be relied upon. An example would be the lack of knowledge in a competitive situation where the basic cause and effect are known such as a competitor's expected product launch can change the future of the business and the market.

   Today's business environment is constantly changing, especially in this new age of technology. There is a need to keep pace with changing times and stay relevant. We, therefore, need to invest in information, which works best in conjunction with structural changes allowing organizations to reduce uncertainty.

3. **Complex:** Many different yet interconnected parts and multiple key decision factors are at play in the integration of diverse agents, emergence, adaptation, coevolution, and weak signals. An example will be when a company operates in many countries, each of which has its own regulatory environment, tariffs, and cultural values. Restructure, bring in or develop specialists, and increase resources adequate to address the complexity.

   Many situations consist of various interconnected parts and variables. Being well informed of all these various parts can be extremely overwhelming and, more often than not, technical too. Organizations should develop specialists who are better capable of dealing with such complex issues. Building upon resources that are adequate enough to address complexity can go far in the success of an organization as well.

4. **Ambiguous:** Open to more than one interpretation—the meaning of an event can be understood in different ways. Causal relationships are completely unclear as no precedent exists, forcing you to face unknown factors. An example will be when a company decides to move into developing markets or to launch new types of products that are outside its previous experience. Companies need to be prepared to take on risk, perhaps initially in trial markets, to evaluate outcomes. Lessons learned can be applied progressively over time to other markets.

   In order to tackle the issue of ambiguity, organizations should experiment and take calculated risks. Generating hypotheses and testing them allows the business to be careful in new ventures, ultimately allowing them to learn from these investments.

Leading in a VUCA world provides not only a challenging environment for leaders to operate and for executive development programs to have an impact but also a much-needed range of new competencies. The new reality is a result of the realization that new and different capabilities are needed to succeed (Bawany 2016a).

# The Fourth Industrial Revolution (Industry 4.0)

Digitization has an impact on all organizations across various sectors or industries. However, the impact is different in each case, which makes it essential for companies to have a good understanding and perception of what challenges they are facing and how digitization will affect their company, that is, which opportunities can be seized and which threats have to be faced (Bawany 2018a).

The impact of digital disruption has to be managed alongside the more general VUCA operating conditions of recent years (Bawany 2016b). An ability to calculate and manage/mitigate risk will, therefore, be another key requirement of leaders seeking to propel their organizations into the digital age. Navigating a course through these difficult conditions may also force leaders to look at their individual leadership styles and decide whether it needs to be adjusted.

Professor Klaus Schwab, the founder and executive chairman of the World Economic Forum (WEF), has published a book entitled *The Fourth Industrial Revolution* in which he describes how this fourth revolution is fundamentally different from the previous three, which were characterized mainly by advances in technology (Schwab 2017).

Schwab describes the first three industrial revolutions as the steam-enabled transport and mechanical production revolution of the late 18th century; the electricity-enabled mass production revolution of the late 19th century; and the computer-enabled technology revolution of the 20th century, which began in the 1960s.

The Fourth Industrial Revolution (or Industry 4.0 as it is more commonly known) represents the combination of AI, robotics, cyberphysical systems, the Internet of Things (IoT), and the Systems of Systems. In short, it is the idea of smart factories in which machines are augmented with web connectivity and connected to a system that can visualize the entire production chain and make decisions on its own. In this fourth revolution, a range of new technologies will evolve that combine the physical, digital, and biological worlds (see Figure 1.2). These new technologies will impact all disciplines, economies, and industries and even challenge our ideas about what it means to be human (Bawany 2018d).

**INDUSTRIAL REVOLUTION**

TRANSFORMING INDUSTRIES AND INNOVATION

**INDUSTRY 1.0**

Mechanization, steam
power, weaving loom

**INDUSTRY 2.0**

Mass production,
assembly line,
electrical energy

**INDUSTRY 3.0**

Automation, computers
and electronics

**INDUSTRY 4.0**

Cyber physical systems,
Internet of things, networks

1784    1870    1969    TODAY

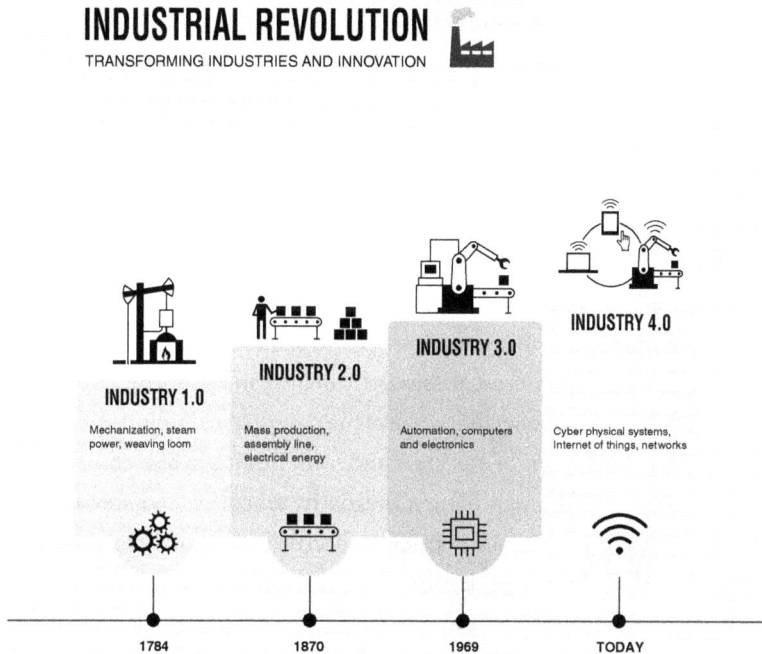

*Figure 1.2  The evolution of the Industrial Revolution*

Technological innovation is on the brink of fueling momentous changes throughout the global economy, generating great benefits and challenges in equal measure. To thrive in this environment, Schwab argues, public–private research collaborations should increase and should be structured toward building knowledge and human capital to the benefit of all.

There will be enormous managerial leadership challenges as the impact of technology and the disruption that follows will result in an exogenous force over which leaders would have little or no control at times. However, it is the role of leaders to guide their teams and to be mindful of these forces when making business decisions that would impact the sustainability of their organizations. They should thus grasp the opportunity and power so as to shape the Fourth Industrial Revolution and direct it toward a future that reflects the organizational values and success.

To do this, however, leaders must develop a comprehensive and collective, shared view of how technology is affecting the lives of their employees and at a macro-level how it is reshaping the economic, social, cultural, and human environments. There has never been a time of greater promise, or one of greater potential peril. Today's leaders and decision makers, however, are too often trapped in traditional, linear thinking, or too absorbed by the multiple crises demanding their attention, to think strategically about the forces of disruption and innovation shaping their organization's future.

In the end, it all comes down to people and values. By putting people first and empowering them, leaders need to shape a future that works for all stakeholders. In its most pessimistic, dehumanized form, the Fourth Industrial Revolution may indeed have the potential to "robotize" humanity and, thus, deprive us of our heart and soul. But it can also complement the best aspects of human nature: creativity, empathy, and stewardship; it can also lift humanity into a new collective and moral consciousness based on a shared sense of destiny. It is therefore incumbent on all of us to make sure the latter prevails.

Leading in Industry 4.0 requires the next-generation leaders to be able to adapt themselves to these new technologies, and to be able to do so effectively the relevant leadership skills and competencies would need to be developed and demonstrated effectively (Bawany, 2019).

# CHAPTER 2

# What Makes a Great NextGen Leader?

## Leadership Challenge from the "New" Business Environment

A topic as complex as what makes a great NextGen or future leader can be viewed from various perspectives and be broken into various elements and each is examined in detail.

Today's turbulent business environment demands that individuals and organizations perform at higher levels and with greater speed than at any time in the past. Organizational leaders and team members alike must place a new emphasis on developing an open and trust-based relationship that will lead to the development of a positive organizational climate and organizational success (Bawany 2018e).

The global environment is increasing the degree of complexity for organizations operating anywhere in the world. With this complexity arises the need for a different kind of inquiry operating within our lives and organizations. The requirement for greater openness to uncertainty will challenge our sense of purpose, identity, and self-efficacy.

Too often in times of turbulence, including in a disruptive, volatile, uncertain, complex, and ambiguous (VUCA) world, the temptation is to "batten down the hatches" and seek safety by focusing on what can be controlled. Typically, this means turning inward and acting "defensively" to avoid damage and minimize risk. Caution and prudence, like most other leadership behaviors, are useful only in conjunction with the exercise of good judgment. In stressful circumstances, leaders need to remember that not all risks are bad, not all opportunities for growth disappear, and a broad, externally focused perspective is more important than ever.

Leaders are facing an almost overwhelming task of restoring confidence and respect in leadership and business. They are being called upon to guide organizations through times of turbulence and uncertainty, to show the way forward, and to set an example—all this in the face of an increasingly disruptive global economy and in a climate of cynicism and mistrust: tough economic and political circumstances by any standards.

Aligning people is about generating awareness and understanding the differences between individuals' preferred ways of working and making decisions or managing relationships, and creating a common understanding, a common sense of purpose, and a shared commitment to action.

Organizations need leaders capable of envisioning the future and motivating, inspiring, and engaging their employees. They should also adapt themselves to the changing needs of both the internal and external stakeholders.

In essence, the heart of the leadership challenge that confronts today's leaders is learning how to lead in situations of ever-greater volatility and uncertainty in a globalized business environment. In addition, leaders need to deal with the increasing scale and complexity of new organizational forms that often break away from traditional organizational models and structures within which many have learned their "leadership trade" (Bawany 2015a).

## Leadership Is a Facet of Management

A useful starting point is to briefly consider the similarities and distinctions between the functions of leadership and management. While, fundamentally, both are concerned with effective goal accomplishment, and both involve influencing the actions of people, leadership and management are distinct concepts. Much has been written on the subject of "leadership versus management," and a detailed examination is beyond the scope of this book. However, the distinction between the two is important to recognize, particularly when seeking to establish interventions intended to shape leadership development and effect organizational culture change.

Leadership and management are two notions that are often used interchangeably. However, these words actually describe two different concepts. We will discuss these differences and explain why both terms are thought to be similar.

With dramatic changes in the business landscape today, organizations must embrace, adapt, and respond quickly to changes, and this reality calls for a new paradigm of leadership. One of the biggest challenges that leaders face is to develop a new mindset that relies on strategic and critical thinking skills along with emotional and social intelligence competencies. This is the hallmark of high-performing leaders, which requires a move from transactional management to transformational leadership in engaging the various stakeholders toward organizational success.

Management and leadership are both important, but it is often difficult for leaders to focus on both dimensions of their job. Traditional management is needed to meet current obligations to customers, shareholders, employees, and others. The problem is that too many people are doing management, with too few providing leadership and fewer still who have integrated the skills and qualities needed for meeting challenges in both leadership and management.

Jack Welch, the legendary former chairman and CEO of General Electric, is one of the best known examples of a business leader who combines good management and effective leadership. He not only understands and practices good management such as cost control but is also a master leader, actively promoting change and communicating a vision, resulting in GE being consistently one of the most successful Fortune 500 organizations throughout his tenure.

The primary aim of a manager has been for a long time (and will continue to be in this era of Industry 4.0) toward maximizing the output of the organization through administrative implementation. To achieve this, managers must undertake the following functions (Fayol 1949; see Figure 2.1):

1. Organization
2. Planning
3. Staffing
4. Leading
5. Controlling

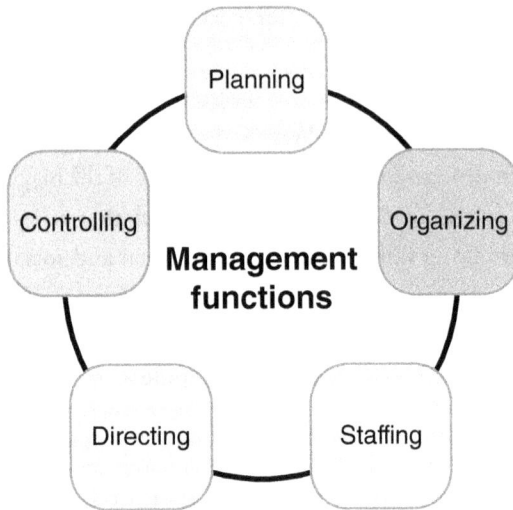

*Figure 2.1  The five basic management functions*

Leadership is an important component of the management function. A manager cannot just be a leader; they also need formal authority to be effective. For any organizational initiative to take effect, senior management must be fully engaged with the organization and act as a role model. This engagement cannot be delegated.

Managers think incrementally, while leaders think radically. Managers do things right, going by the book and adhering to company policy, whereas leaders do the right thing, seeking out the truth and making decisions based on fact, not prejudice. Oftentimes, they stand out by being different—questioning assumptions and showing a preference for innovation.

Warren Bennis further explicated a dichotomy between managers and leaders. He drew 12 distinctions between the two groups (Bennis 1989):

1. Managers administer, leaders innovate
2. Managers ask how, leaders ask what and why
3. Managers focus on systems, leaders focus on people
4. Managers do things right, leaders do the right things
5. Managers maintain, leaders develop
6. Managers rely on control, leaders inspire trust

7. Managers have a short-term perspective, leaders have a longer-term perspective
8. Managers accept the status quo, leaders challenge the status quo
9. Managers have an eye on the bottom line, leaders have an eye on the horizon
10. Managers imitate, leaders originate
11. Managers emulate the classic good soldier, leaders are their own person
12. Managers copy, leaders show originality.

## Who Are the NextGen Leaders?

Baby boomers are stepping into retirement in growing numbers. This means that companies are starting to lose institutional knowledge and experience, not to mention an entire section of leadership. While there is still time to get younger generations of high-potential employees up to speed on managerial leadership tasks, it is crucial to remember that executive development, including training and coaching, is not something that should be an afterthought but a carefully planned and calibrated strategy to ensure the sustainability of the organization.

The current leadership needs to identify potential leaders and allow them to make decisions about important tasks while coaching and mentoring them through the leadership challenges that the baby boomers have been through. Preparing for an effective leadership transition will ensure that potential pitfalls are foreseen and avoided, making way for a smoother change of hands later.

While business and human resource leaders seek to understand the generational shifts in the global workforce on a macro-level, at the micro-level (the focus of this book), organizations need to reexamine their human resource and talent management strategies. They need to focus on the readiness and development of their high-potential NextGen leaders for the era of Industry 4.0 to lead high-performance teams and organizations. Sustained efforts are needed in the following areas:

1. Identification, assessment, and selection of high-potential leaders
2. Provision of developmental support (including coaching, mentoring, and training).

## Who Are High-Potential NextGen Leaders?

The identification, assessment, selection, and development of NextGen leaders, including the high-potential leaders, is a cornerstone of the talent strategy of many leading and successful organizations.

If an organization can identify early on those with high potential for leadership among its human resources, it can concentrate resources on developing these people to help them realize their potential. Through this process, it can efficiently build up a leadership bench strength and a pipeline of talent who can eventually become the leaders of the organization. While this is a sensible objective, Konczak and Foster (2009) found that organizations generally lack a clear definition for high potentials and even program goals and objectives.

In a study that Ready, Conger, and Hill (2010) conducted, as much as 98 percent of the 45 organizations surveyed reported having a process for identifying *high potentials*. However, Silzer and Church (2009a), in a separate study, found that there was no clear, universal definition of *potential*, and some organizations relied on definitions that are not backed by well-grounded research. In particular, many organizations define *potential* according to the perceived likelihood of progression to a specific higher level in the organization. Such definitions are so vague that they could be subject to different interpretations, and different managers may rely on different criteria for identifying the high potentials.

In addition, a common misperception of managers, human resource practitioners, and even high potentials themselves is to equate high performers with high potentials (Dries and Pepermans 2008; Martin and Schmidt 2010; Silzer and Church 2009b). As a result, it is not uncommon for organizations to rely on past and current performance data to identify high potentials even though these individuals are moving to positions that may have significantly different demands and thus require a different set of behaviors and skill sets for effective performance.

What is clear from the work of a number of researchers in this field is that high potentials are not the same as high performers.

Nonetheless, potential and performance are related in that a higher level of potential tends to support a higher level of performance, and strong performance is often what helps high potentials to get noticed in the first place. Thus, it is not surprising to find that most high potentials are high performers (Martin and Schmidt 2010; Ready, Conger, and Hill 2010).

However, not all high performers are high potentials. Research by the Corporate Leadership Council of more than 20,000 high-potential employees in more than 100 organizations worldwide revealed that only about 30 percent of high performers are high potentials (Martin and Schmidt 2010). What distinguishes high potentials is that unlike high performers who are merely defined by their effectiveness in their current role, high potentials possess the qualities to be effective in roles involving broader responsibilities at higher levels in the organizational hierarchy, and the roles are to be assumed within the next 3 to 10 years or longer timeframe (Silzer and Church 2009a).

According to Ram Charan (2017), who is a highly acclaimed business advisor and best-selling author of several books on developing the leadership pipeline of high potentials, "Everyone has potential to grow, but not everyone, not even every person with leadership skills, has the potential to lead a large, complex organization in the near and distant future. Amidst everything that is new and different, today's high potential leaders, or 'HiPos', must be able to 'identify the untapped opportunities their companies will pursue that will mobilize the organization'" to meet the forthcoming needs.

How inclusive or exclusive should organizations be when developing employee talents? In a world of unlimited resources, organizations would surely invest in everyone. After all, as Henry Ford is credited as saying, "the only thing worse than training your employees and having them leave is not training them and having them stay." In the real world, however, limited budgets force organizations to be much more selective, which explains the growing interest in high-potential identification. An employee's potential sets the upper limits of their development range—the more potential they have, the quicker and cheaper it is to develop them.

In line with Pareto's principle, these studies show that across a wide range of tasks, industries, and organizations, a small proportion of the workforce tends to drive a large proportion of organizational results, such that:

- the top 1 percent accounts for 10 percent of the organizational output
- the top 5 percent accounts for 25 percent of the organizational output
- the top 20 percent accounts for 80 percent of the organizational output.

Chamorro-Premuzic and his coauthors in a *Harvard Business Review* article state that

> Scientific studies have long suggested that investing in the right people will maximize organizations' returns. In a world of unlimited resources, organizations would surely invest in everyone. In the real world, however, limited budgets force organizations to be much more selective, which explains the growing interest in high potential (HiPo) identification. If we are going to invest in the right employees, how do we find them? What are the key indicators that signal star potential? (Chamorro-Premuzic, Adler, and Kaiser 2017)

## Attributes of High Potentials

A survey of the current research and perspectives on high potentials (e.g., Bawany 2015b; Bolt and Hagemann 2009; Campbell and Smith 2010; Chamorro-Premuzic, Adler, and Kaiser 2017; Charan, Drotter, and Noel 2001; Corporate Leadership Council 2005; Gallup 2018; Hagemann and Bawany 2016; Ready, Conger, and Hill 2010; Silzer and Church 2009a) indicates that these qualities include a combination of variables such as ability, drive/motivation, engagement, learning agility, and social skills (part of the suite of emotional and social intelligence competencies).

## Ability

The abilities identified are typically based on the success profile of current leaders and/or the expected profile of future leaders and tend to be fairly broad and generic, as the high potentials are not being selected for a particular target position but for a range of possible leadership positions. Intellectual abilities are almost always included as an important attribute because top leaders need the cognitive capacity to deal with complex business challenges.

Ability here refers to indicators as to whether an individual is able to do the job in question. The best indicator for leadership ability here is demonstrating the knowledge and skill it takes to perform the key tasks that make up the job. The single best predictor of job performance is a work sample test, where one can observe the candidate actually performing the tasks that make up the job.

However, in forecasting potential to excel in a bigger, more complex job at some point in the future, the question shifts to assessing how likely an individual is able to learn and master the requisite knowledge and skill. The single best predictor of this is IQ or cognitive ability. Learning ability includes not only a substantial cognitive component but also the motivation to pick up new knowledge and skills quickly and in a flexible manner.

Any role requires abilities beyond cognitive ability. For instance, the potential for performing in a leadership role at the executive level requires cognitive readiness skills, including critical thinking, strategic thinking, complex problem solving, and decision making, as well as the ability to reinvent the organization to ensure its survival in the long term. Others crucial skills required are vision, innovative, and imagination as well as an entrepreneurial mindset. Thus, early indicators of the ability for senior organizational leadership may also include creativity and a knack for systems thinking.

Personality-related interpersonal and emotional skills are important, too, as leaders have to manage themselves and work with a range of people and work through other people. In particular, they need to be able to lead a team, which entails having the skills to manage, inspire, support, and develop others in order to get the best out of them. Emotional resilience, an established predictor of long-term leadership success, is also commonly included as a key attribute because it helps leaders to deal with stressful situations. In addition, high potentials may be required to possess sound technical skills in their career field or relevant business knowledge. Essentially, these are skills and knowledge that will help them to succeed in their chosen career.

## Drive/Motivation

While ability is necessary, it is not a sufficient condition for being considered high potentials. Individuals may possess the ability but may not be motivated to make use of their ability to perform on the job. Thus, in addition to ability, it is widely agreed that high potentials need to be driven to excel and achieve results. At the same time, beyond being motivated to excel in their current job (which could characterize high performers equally well), high potentials have a strong desire to lead and to advance in their career. This aspiration is important, as the key to spurring the high potentials is for them to put in the necessary effort to strive for, take on, and succeed in progressively higher level leadership positions. This also means that high potentials are more likely to take the initiative to pursue career opportunities and relevant developmental challenges.

High potentials demonstrate the will and motivation to work hard, achieve, and do whatever it takes to get the job done. It is easily identified as work ethic and ambition—an ability to remain dissatisfied with one's achievements. This deeply motivational mindset is the accelerator that multiplies the potential influence of ability and social skills on the future success. Ability and social skill may be considered talent, but the potential is talent multiplied by the drive, as this will determine how much ability and social skills are put to use.

Drive can be assessed by standardized tests that measure conscientiousness, achievement motivation, and ambition. It can also be identified behaviorally—as signaled by how hard an individual works, willingness to take on extra duties and assignments, eagerness for more responsibility, and even readiness to sacrifice. For instance, many executive-level roles require a global mindset and some degree of cross-cultural experience. The willingness to embrace a degree of psychological and even physical discomfort (maybe even relocate in order to gain the experience and develop these skills) separates mere talented individuals from those who are truly high potentials.

## Engagement

The "high potential" distinction is meaningful only within the context of an organization. An organization identifies high potentials because it wants to groom them to be future leaders. Hence, it is important that the organization identifies people who are likely to stay with the organization over the long term. Thus, another attribute of high potentials is that they should feel a sense of engagement toward the organization and be committed toward its mission and values. This is particularly important in this day and age when people typically have a greater range of career choices (Silzer and Church 2009a) and, thus, are less likely to stay with a single organization throughout their working life (Erickson 2010).

Employee engagement and retention is a constant struggle for businesses all over the world. In fact, according to data from Gallup, "87% of employees worldwide are not engaged." An engaged employee is more likely to stay with an organization, produce a strong performance as a leader, and inspire others to action than a disengaged employee (Gallup 2018).

Some of the hallmarks of an engaged employee to look for when assessing leadership candidates include:

- *Passion for your company's industry.* How enthusiastic is the employee about the industry your company serves? Leaders set the tone for their teams, and their enthusiasm or reticence will spread to others quickly, affecting performance.
- *Engaged in the workplace.* How often does the employee go above and beyond the minimum requirements of their job? Engaged employees will volunteer to task forces and projects and work harder and take ownership of their work to make sure it is completed in the right way the first time.

- *Acting as an ambassador for your company.* When interacting with others, does the employee represent your company in a positive light? Do they mentor junior employees or help with the onboarding process of new employees? Employees who are engaged enough with your company's brand to recommend the company to their circle of friends as both a great place to work and an example of the best traits of your industry are more likely to stay with the company and inspire others to do their best work.

Highly engaged employees aren't just productive—they show everyone around them the best traits of your business, which inspires others to be more productive as well.

### Learning Agility

Learning agility is the ability to incorporate new material quickly. It has been found that the ability to learn quickly and use that information in business was the strongest predictor of success. Those with agility show strong leadership qualities. Only about one-third of high-potential employees live up to their promise, but those with various dimensions of learning agility perform at the highest rate. These skills can be developed and improved. Those with various agilities learn quickly from information and experience, take risks, strive for growth, and exhibit resiliency. These people absorb information through books and classes, peer learning, direct experience, and reflections on past performances. Even failure can prove valuable to those with agility because they learn and adapt quickly from their unsuccessful experiences.

The seminal research in this area was conducted three decades ago by McCall, Lombardo, and Morrison (1988). In their groundbreaking book entitled *Lessons of Experience*, the authors discovered that many managers who produced positive results on the basis of their current technical skills did not perform well after they were promoted. They found that numerous managers and executives derailed because they tended to depend largely on the same skills that got them promoted in the first place rather than learning new ones. The strengths that used to work became weaknesses when they relied too heavily on them or applied them when the context was inappropriate. In contrast, the successful ones (i.e., the high potentials) seemed comfortable with new, different, and challenging situations. These managers and executives were willing to learn and develop from their "lessons of experience."

In another research entitled "Learning Agility as a Prime Indicator of Potential," the authors hypothesized that high potentials with a higher level of learning agility would perform better once they had been promoted. Indeed, this hypothesis was borne out of the finding that more successful leaders were those who scored higher on the levels of learning agility after they were promoted (Eichinger and Lombardo 2004). They highlight four types of learning agility:

1. **Mental agility:** they are excellent critical thinkers who are comfortable with complexity, examine problems carefully, and make fresh connections.
2. **People agility:** they know themselves very well and can readily deal with a wide variety of people and tough situations.
3. **Change agility:** they are curious, like to experiment, and can effectively deal with the discomfort of change.
4. **Results agility:** they deliver results in first-time situations by inspiring teams and exhibit the sort of presence that builds confidence both in themselves and in others.

### Social Intelligence Skills

There is a growing significance of teamwork and collaboration in leading high-performance organizations. At a basic level, all employees should be able to get along and earn the support of supervisors and coworkers.

The life of a leader has plenty of demands and pressures. Having the skills to handle them is a prerequisite for success. From the ongoing longitudinal research by the Centre for Executive Education (CEE), we have identified several specific skills from a wide array of emotional and social intelligence competencies, such as the ones that differentiate successful leaders from other people. Fortunately for high potentials, these skills can be improved with appropriate executive development support, including training and coaching (Bawany 2015b).

Research has shown that most successful leaders have strengths in demonstrating emotional intelligence competencies. Emotional intelligence is the ability to manage ourselves and our relationships effectively, and it consists of four fundamental capabilities: self-awareness, self-management, social awareness, and social skill. Each capability, in turn, is composed of specific sets of competencies (Goleman 2000).

Social skills involve two fundamental abilities: the ability to manage yourself and the ability to manage others (relationships). Employees willing to succeed in bigger, more complex jobs should first be able to manage themselves—to handle increased pressure, deal constructively with adversity, and act with dignity and integrity. Second, they are able to establish and maintain cooperative working relationships, build a broad network of contacts and form alliances, and be influential and persuasive with a range of different stakeholders. And for senior roles, they have to be able to develop sophisticated political skills—the ability to read an audience, decode the unspoken rules, and find solutions that satisfy the often competing interests of key powerbrokers.

Goleman defines *social intelligence* as being knowledgeable about both our interpersonal relationships and also how we act in them (Goleman 2006). These include:

1. **Visionary leadership:** the ability to take charge and inspire with a compelling vision.
2. **Influence:** the ability to wield a range of persuasive tactics.
3. **Developing others:** the propensity to bolster the abilities of others through feedback and guidance.
4. **Communication:** skill at listening and at sending clear, convincing, and well-tuned messages.
5. **Change catalyst:** proficiency in initiating new ideas and leading people in a new direction.
6. **Conflict management:** the ability to de-escalate disagreements and orchestrate resolutions.

7. **Building bonds:** proficiency at cultivating and maintaining a web of relationships.
8. **Teamwork and collaboration:** competence at promoting cooperation and building teams.

The ability to manage oneself as well as others is the core element of emotional and social intelligence that can be assessed by psychometric assessment tools and further refined through training and development.

# CHAPTER 3

# Leading High-Performance Organization

## Introduction

Organizations today face unprecedented challenges operating in a global environment that is increasingly volatile, uncertain, complex, and ambiguous (VUCA). Leaders are also confronted with increased competition, globalization, demand for growing social responsibilities, and a stream of technological revolutions causing disruption in the marketplace. The turbulence in the business environment demands that individuals and organizations perform at higher levels and with greater speed than at any time in the past. Organizations need leaders to visualize the future, motivate and inspire employees, and adapt to changing needs of both the internal and external stakeholders.

In a high-performance organization (HPO), a "can-do and true believer" mentality prevails. Everyone believes in the vision and mission and demonstrates the values of the organization. People put the organization above themselves, team, or department, as they believe that they are involved in something bigger than simply their own self-interest. They have a strong sense of purpose and values, identify with the organization, and act as if they are the owners. Employees of Disney, Southwest Airlines, and Starbucks are some good examples. They have a reason to work, and they show this each and every day. That is the hallmark of HPOs.

But what or who is influencing these employees and aligning their behaviors? Aligning people is about generating awareness and understanding of the differences between individuals in the way they prefer to work and the way they make decisions or manage relationships. By creating a common understanding, a common sense of purpose and a shared commitment to action evolve.

Organizational leaders and employees alike must place a new emphasis on developing an open and trust-based relationship that will lead to the development of a positive organizational climate and organizational success (Bawany 2014a).

In essence, the heart of the leadership challenge that confronts today's leaders is learning how to lead in situations of ever-greater volatility and uncertainty in a globalized business environment. This is compounded by the need to deal with scale, complexity, and new organizational forms that often break with the traditional organizational models and structures from which the earlier model of leadership may have been learned (Bawany 2015a). Hence, leaders need to challenge their mental models in their efforts to build and sustain an HPO (Bawany 2018c).

## Characteristics or Profile of HPOs

HPOs are the role models of the business world. They are being benchmarked by other organizations as they provide or represent real-world versions of a modern managerial ideal: the organization that is so excellent in so many areas that it consistently outperforms most of its competitors in the same industry over extended periods of time. Leaders want to know more about HPOs so they can apply the best practice approaches and lessons learned to their own companies. Of course, the goal is to ensure that their own organizations excel in the marketplace.

In 1982, when Tom Peters and Bob Waterman published *In Search of Excellence*, the idea of comparing, identifying, and analyzing the best-performing organizations came into vogue (Kirby 2005). Since that time, many studies have used comparison techniques to tease out what sets HPOs apart. In his book *Built to Last*, Jim Collins (1994) took a somewhat similar approach. Many business leaders have tried to adopt the practices of the companies profiled in these two books.

But the goal of identifying the most durable high performers through comparison is a difficult one to achieve. One of the problems is that sustaining high performance is a major challenge for any organization across all industries. Interestingly, many of the organizations that were profiled were unable to sustain the high performance.

For years, researchers have been trying to identify and study HPOs. Much has been learned during this time. As Julia Kirby (2005) noted in the *Harvard Business Review*, management experts continue to build on one another's work in order to formulate more sophisticated ideas about organizational performance.

The various research works published, including that of André A. de Waal (2007) and American Management Association (2007) report on "The High-Performance Organization Survey 2007," provide insights into the characteristics of HPOs. Generally speaking, HPOs are superior to their low-performance counterparts in the following areas:

1. **Strategy**
   a. They define a strong vision that excites and challenges, based on a winning strategy that is clear and well-thought-out. Their mission, vision, values, and operating philosophies are consistent with their strategy.
   b. They balance long-term focus and short-term focus to safeguard the long-term continuity of the business and its contribution to the world. At the same time, they achieve short-term results as well, which makes it possible to plan for the future.
   c. They set clear, ambitious, measurable, and achievable goals, which raises the level of aspiration and creates a sense of stretch.
   d. They create clarity and a common understanding of the organization's mission, direction, and strategy that is understood by everyone within the organization.
   e. They align strategy, goals, and objectives with the demands of the external environment, so corporate renewal is always based on customer needs.
   f. They adopt the strategy that will set the company apart by developing many new options and alternatives to compensate for redundant strategies.
   g. They adhere to high ethical standards throughout the organization.
   h. They create an organizational design and structure that complement the intended business strategy.
   i. They stimulate cross-functional and cross-organizational collaboration by making teamwork and collaboration top priorities of

management. They foster teamwork by stressing the importance of teams for the performance of the organization and develop a team feeling by creating team commitment, getting everyone on the same team, and establishing shared responsibility.

j.  They simplify and flatten the organization by reducing the boundaries and barriers between and around units, thus getting rid of bureaucracy and organizational complexity.

k.  They foster organization-wide sharing of information, knowledge, and best practices by creating the infrastructure and incentives for these.

l.  They continuously realign the business with changing internal and external circumstances by setting up an adaptable business model that can be easily altered on the basis of opportunities in the external environment and shifts in customer needs and market conditions.

2.  **Leadership**

a.  In an HPO, trust-based relationships are maintained with employees at all levels. This is strengthened because loyalty is valued, smart people are treated in a smart manner, people are shown respect, and a learning attitude is fostered. Also, individual relationships between managers and employees are created and maintained, both leaders and employees are encouraged to believe and trust each other, and people are treated fairly.

b.  Leaders live with integrity and demonstrate ontological humility. They lead by example, being honest and sincere and showing commitment, enthusiasm, and respect. They have a strong set of ethics and standards, have credibility, and consistently maintain a sense of vulnerability by not being arrogant.

c.  They make decisive, action-focused decision by avoiding over-analysis but coming up with decisions and effective actions, while at the same time fostering action-taking by others.

d.  They coach and facilitate the development of employees by being supportive, helping them, protecting them from outside interference, and being available.

e.  Leaders stretch themselves and their people by setting high standards, stretching goals, and continuously raising the performance bar.

f. They demonstrate a repertoire of situational leadership styles that are effective in communicating the organization's values and by making sure the strategy has been received and embraced by organizational members.

g. They allow experiments and mistakes by permitting taking risks, being willing to take risks themselves, and seeing mistakes as an opportunity to learn and quickly innovate.

h. They inspire people to accomplish extraordinary results by demonstrating charismatic leadership, creating a larger-than-life mindset, inspiring all to do their best, and mobilizing individual initiative.

i. They develop or grow leaders within their organization by encouraging people to become leaders, filling positions with internal talent, and promoting from within.

j. They stimulate change and improvement by continuously striving for self-awareness and renewal, developing dynamic managerial capabilities to enhance flexibility, and by being personally involved in change activities.

k. They recruit and leverage on a diverse and complementary management team and workforce to help spot the inefficiencies of their operations and create a climate that supports innovation and creativity in solving workplace challenges.

l. They are committed to the organization for the long haul by balancing common purpose with self-interest and teaching organizational members to put the needs of the enterprise first.

m. They hold employees responsible for results and are decisive about nonperformers by keeping their focus on the achievement of results and maintaining, at the same time, clear accountability for performance and making tough decisions.

3. **Customer**

a. They go above and beyond to delight their customers through distinctively branded customer experience.

b. They strive to be world class in providing customers value, think hard about customers' future and long-term needs, and exceed customer expectations.

    c. They are more likely to leverage on data analytics and on their customer information as the most important factor for developing new products and services.

    d. They continuously strive to enhance customer value creation by learning what customers want, understanding their values, and building excellent relationships with them. They have direct contact with customers, engaging them, being responsive, and focusing on continuously enhancing customer value.

    e. They maintain good and long-term relationships not only with their customers but also with all stakeholders by networking broadly, being generous to society, and creating mutually beneficial opportunities and win–win relationships.

    f. They continuously monitor the VUCA business environment and proactively respond to shifts and opportunities in the marketplace, by surveying the markets to understand the context of the business, identifying trends and exploring scenarios, capturing external information quickly and accurately, anticipating adversaries through careful study and assessment, and creating a warning system to spot changes to which the organization must respond quickly, so as to ensure that all stakeholders' expectations, particularly those of the customers, are met.

4. **Employees**

    a. They empower employees and give them the freedom to decide and act by decentralizing decision-making authority and giving autonomy to organizational members to operate within clearly established boundaries and constraints of what is allowed and what is not.

    b. They are superior in terms of clarifying performance measures, training employees to do their jobs, and enabling employees to work well together.

    c. They create a culture of transparency, openness, and trust by establishing a shared understanding, openly sharing information, and fostering informality, yet remaining focused on goals.

    d. Their employees are more likely to think the organization is a good place to work.

    e. They emphasize on readiness to meet new challenges and are committed to innovation.

    f. They encourage employees to use their skills, knowledge, and experience to create unique solutions for customers.

    g. Their high-performance teams have a shared purpose and values that serve as an operating philosophy, enabling them to be adaptable and respond quickly, as necessary, to changes in the environment. Their teams use creativity and outside-the-box thinking in creating innovative resolutions to business challenges.

5. **Organizational Culture and Climate**

    a. They create a culture that empowers employees to operate within clearly established boundaries and constraints of what is allowed and what is not.

    b. They establish clear, strong, and meaningful core values and make sure they are widely shared and accepted within the company.

    c. They develop and maintain a performance-driven culture by fighting inertia and complacency, challenging the enemies of a winning mindset, focusing strongly on getting high excellence in whatever the organization does, and stimulating employees to achieve high performance.

    d. They create a culture of transparency, openness, and trust by establishing shared understanding, openly sharing information, and fostering informality and are committed to goals.

    e. They create a learning organization by continuously investing in training and upgrading of skills, establishing good management development and top-of-the-line training programs, and constantly identifying and accessing new competencies.

    f. They attract exceptional potential employees with a can-do attitude who fit the culture, nurture highly talented employees, and give bright employees space to change and excel.

    g. They engage and involve employees in developing vision and values and in interactive discussions and decision-making processes and communicate issues and developments important to the organization.

    h. They create a safe and secure workplace by giving employees a sense of safety (physical and psychological), including job security, and by not indiscriminately laying off employees (until it can no longer be avoided).

i.   They master the core competencies. They are innovators themselves. They decide and stick to what the company does best, keeping core competencies inside the firm and outsourcing non-core competencies.

j.   They develop employees to be resilient and flexible and recruit a workforce with maximum flexibility.

k.   They align employee behavior and values with company values and direction at all organizational levels by translating vision into local objectives and letting individuals realize that they have accountabilities and obligations both to themselves and to the organization.

## The HPO Framework for Industry 4.0

Leading in Industry 4.0 that is highly disruptive as well as volatile, uncertain, complex, and ambiguous provides a challenging environment for leaders to operate and for executive development programs to have an impact. It also brings forth a much-needed new range of competencies. The new environment has resulted in the necessity for new and different capabilities for organizations to succeed (Bawany 2018e).

We are operating in a hypercompetitive VUCA business environment. The world moves faster today when compared with 20 to 30 years ago. Companies feel the pressure to decrease time to market and improve the quality of products while delivering ever-changing customer expectations to maintain competitive posture, that is, be adaptive and nimble. Deriving results in HPOs has become more and more difficult even for companies with dedicated and knowledgeable employees in their workforce and business leaders to leverage.

A research by the Centre for Executive Education (CEE) found that various leadership competencies are crucial in deriving results and achieving organizational success in an HPO operating in a highly disruptive and increasingly VUCA-driven business environment (Bawany 2016a). These include cognitive readiness (critical and strategic thinking skills), emotional and social intelligence (ESI), managerial coaching and leading team for performance, effective negotiation and conflict management, and cross-cultural communication and diversity management.

The business environment is changing constantly, and a leader must respond in kind in the effort toward the development to be an HPO (see Figure 3.1). Leaders need to challenge their mental models in their efforts to build and sustain an HPO (Bawany 2018c).

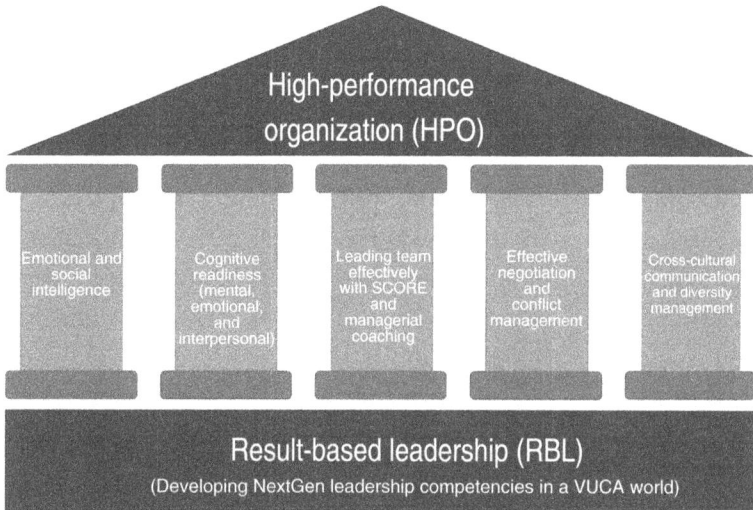

High-performance
organization (HPO)

Emotional and social intelligence

Cognitive readiness (mental, emotional, and interpersonal)

Leading team effectively with SCORE and managerial coaching

Effective negotiation and conflict management

Cross-cultural communication and diversity management

Result-based leadership (RBL)
(Developing NextGen leadership competencies in a VUCA world)

*Figure 3.1  The high-performance organization*

## The Results-Based Leadership Framework

There is currently extensive published research on the direct link between leadership effectiveness and sustained organizational performance. Hence, managerial leadership capability should be of primary concern for all organizations since the contribution and motivation of the employees are key toward achieving the organizational goals and objectives. While the organization needs a financial resource, technical and professional knowledge and expertise, and relevant systems and processes, success cannot be assured and sustained unless the leaders are able to utilize these resources creatively and effectively. Arguably, the organizations that are best placed to survive and thrive in the disruptive business environment of the future Industry 4.0 are those that have a strong focus on leadership development practices and a good understanding of what effective leadership means to them.

The organization's current and NextGen leaders must focus on effectively engaging all stakeholders, in particular, the employees, in delivering results. In the Industry 4.0 era and at a time of continued, significant transitions and challenges, leaders at all levels have a responsibility to ensure that their organization's mission and purpose are at the heart of what they do.

The concept of "engagement" can be defined in many ways. Essentially, engagement is a measure of how an organization values its employees and how employees value their organization and recognize that every individual is at liberty to decide whether to do the minimum required of them or to do more. Engagement can also be taken to represent the degree of empowerment to which staff are involved in decision making and/or the openness and perceived effectiveness of communication. Hence, leaders at all levels have a key role in cultivating a strong culture of engagement.

This, in essence, is the foundation of the "Results-Based Leadership" (RBL) framework (see Figure 3.2).

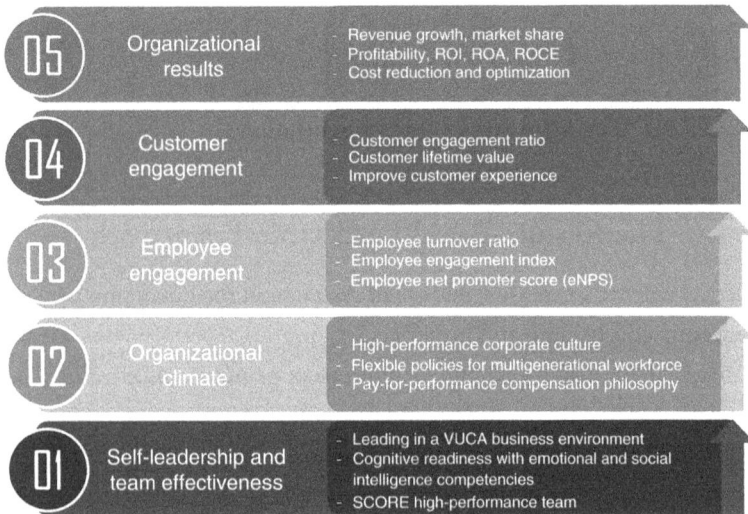

| 05 | Organizational results | - Revenue growth, market share<br>- Profitability, ROI, ROA, ROCE<br>- Cost reduction and optimization |
| 04 | Customer engagement | - Customer engagement ratio<br>- Customer lifetime value<br>- Improve customer experience |
| 03 | Employee engagement | - Employee turnover ratio<br>- Employee engagement index<br>- Employee net promoter score (eNPS) |
| 02 | Organizational climate | - High-performance corporate culture<br>- Flexible policies for multigenerational workforce<br>- Pay-for-performance compensation philosophy |
| 01 | Self-leadership and team effectiveness | - Leading in a VUCA business environment<br>- Cognitive readiness with emotional and social intelligence competencies<br>- SCORE high-performance team |

*Figure 3.2  The RBL framework*

**Step 1:** The basic premise of the RBL framework is that a highly effective transformational leader would start with a strong sense of self-leadership, developing in particular a high level of self-awareness of their own strengths and area of development in the crucial NextGen leadership competencies. These include

ESI along with cognitive (mental) readiness in leading in the highly disruptive, digital, and increasingly VUCA-driven business environment. Next, they need to lead and engage the team by coaching them to success by adopting the proven SCORE High-Performance Team framework that is discussed in Chapter 6.

**Step 2:** Organizational climate (sometimes known as corporate climate) simply refers to how employees feel about working in the organization. Organizational climate is the process of quantifying the culture of an organization. It is a set of characteristics of the work environment, perceived directly or indirectly by the employees that are assumed to be a major force in influencing employee behavior and engagement. By implementing Step 1 effectively along with the relevant human resource practices, the leader will create an organizational climate of trust between themselves and the employees who are highly engaged and would want to remain in the organization.

**Step 3:** The level of employee engagement is dependent on the organizational climate. Employees who are engaged and motivated are instrumental in delivering the required customer service experience for the client that will result in customer engagement and retention. A consequence of the engaged employees is employee loyalty, which will reduce attrition and, thus, costs of hiring new staff.

**Step 4:** Employees who feel fully committed to the organization take great pride in doing their job. They do more than what is expected of them and go that extra mile. In so doing, engaged employees, in particular, the frontline service staff, will have an impact and inevitably influence the buying behavior of customers. The excitement of an engaged employee is contagious and cannot help but rub off on the customer.

**Step 5:** The key performance indicators (KPIs) or metrics of success for the organization differ from one organization to another. However, one of the factors driving the profitability and efficiency is the level of customer engagement or loyalty, since the cost of acquisition of new customers is reduced significantly. Loyalty is a direct result of customer satisfaction. Satisfaction is largely influenced by the value of services provided to customers. Value is created by satisfied, loyal, and productive employees, especially the customer-interfacing service employees. Employee satisfaction, in turn, results primarily from the internal high-quality support services and organizational policies that enable the frontline team to deliver excellent service to customers.

Managers often fail to appreciate how profoundly the organizational climate can influence financial results. It can account for nearly a third of financial performance. Organizational climate, in turn, is influenced by leadership style and the manner in which the leader motivates direct reports, gathers and uses information, makes decisions, manages change initiatives, and handles crises.

The fundamental goal is that organizations must strive to continuously deliver service value and build good customer relationships in order to generate sustainable results through satisfied and loyal customers. Employees being at the forefront of the service delivery chain hold the key to building this satisfied and loyal customer base.

## Competencies for Leading in an HPO for Industry 4.0

The once identifiable boundaries of our marketplaces and industries have now become permeable. They shift continuously, sometimes slowly, sometimes quickly, and always give us the feeling that they are slightly beyond our grasp. In this new business environment, leaders must realize that a sustainable future is only possible if organizations can sense, adapt, and respond to change and if they can help their organizations reinvent themselves in an evolving and rapidly changing world.

Leading in the future has seen a common theme emerge—managing challenges in a business environment that is disrupted and predominantly digital. Technological advancements in artificial intelligence (AI), robotics, sharing platforms, and the Internet-of-Things are fundamentally altering business models and industries. These changes are often not only alien to businesses but also taking place at an unprecedented speed. How do we equip and transform the next generation of leaders with the relevant skills and competencies to meet these challenges?

Today, a new set of digital business and working skills are needed. Companies should focus more heavily on career strategies, talent mobility, and organizational ecosystems and networks to facilitate both individual and organizational reinvention. The problem is not simply one of *reskilling* or planning new and better careers. Instead, organizations must look at leadership, structures, diversity, technology, and the overall employee experience in new and exciting ways.

The reality remains that VUCA world is not going to disappear anytime soon. In fact, it will intensify in the years to come. The chaotic *new normal* in business is real. The global financial crisis of 2008 to 2009 has rendered many business models obsolete, as organizations from various industries throughout the world fell into turbulent environments. In addition, many businesses have been impacted extremely by technological developments such as social media, which has exploded, as well as an aging workforce in some economies, rapid growth of population in many countries, and global disasters that have disrupted lives, economies, and businesses.

This *new normal* VUCA environment is impacting organizations to the extent that their leaders' current set of skills and competencies may no longer be relevant to driving the organization to success. There is a need to continually reassess their readiness and develop the necessary set of competencies for them to lead in this volatile, unpredictable landscape. Leadership agility and adaptability with cognitive readiness are crucial leadership skills that organizations require to succeed in this VUCA world.

It is evident that the impact of the technological change will continue unabated given the constant shifting of the various forces in the business environment. Leading in VUCA times has become increasingly about creating moments of clarity and focus while being proactive and keeping an eye on what is shifting and being prepared to respond to it. Reacting without having any vision leaves employees feeling confused and demotivated.

The Trends in Executive Development Survey has been conducted by Executive Development Associates (EDA) approximately every two years since the early 1980s, and it was in 2016, for the first time, that creating a compelling vision and engaging others around it became the number one trend (Hagemann and Bawany 2016). This finding is consistent in the 2019 Executive Development Trends survey (Hagemann and Bawany 2019).

In the book *Leading with Vision: The Leader's Blueprint for Creating a Compelling Vision and Engaging the Workforce*, Bonnie Hagemann, the CEO of EDA, and her coauthors identified the crucial business challenge today—that leaders are facing a ruthless, competitive climate, and to navigate a successful route through the VUCA era requires a new, more thoughtful, and relevant approach. The rapid changes will most likely accelerate. With this comes the need to constantly adjust course and adapt to be agile and purposeful and to engage and develop the talents of everyone in the business (Hagemann, Vetter, and Maketa 2017).

The quantitative and qualitative research indicates that there is a better and much more effective way to do this going forward, one that will ensure higher returns for organizations in talent, innovation, and competitiveness. One way is to connect the hearts of the employees to the vision or mission of the organization and to ensure that they understand their role and feel being a part of bringing it to reality.

## Developing the VUCA Prime Leadership Competencies

The VUCA model is helpful in identifying the internal and external conditions that affect organizations today. The VUCA prime model developed by Robert Johansen, distinguished fellow at the Institute for the Future, flips the VUCA model and focuses on the characteristics and skills business leaders must develop to counter the effects of a VUCA environment. Johansen proposes that the best VUCA leaders have a vision, understanding, clarity, and agility (Johansen 2011).

In the VUCA prime model, volatility can be countered with vision because vision is even more vital in turbulent times. Leaders with a clear vision of where they want their organizations to be can better weather volatile environmental changes such as economic downturns or new competition. They can make better business decisions that counter the turbulence while keeping the organization's vision in mind.

Uncertainty can be countered with understanding and the ability to stop, look, and listen. To be effective in a VUCA environment, leaders must learn to look and listen beyond their functional areas to make sense of the volatility and to lead with vision. Complexity can be countered with clarity, which is the process of trying to make sense of the chaos. In a VUCA world, chaos comes swift and hard. Leaders who can quickly and clearly tune into all of the minutiae associated with the chaos can make better, more informed business decisions. Finally, ambiguity can be countered with agility. Vision, understanding, clarity, and agility are not mutually exclusive in the VUCA prime model. Rather, they are intertwined elements that help managers become stronger VUCA leaders.

## NextGen Leadership Competencies

There are two things we can say with certainty about the future: It will be different, and it will surprise. Now, more than ever, leaders are compelled to navigate unfamiliar, challenging times, a quickening pace of change, increasing expectations, and a rising tide of rapidly evolving conditions. This new and different environment is challenging leaders to find new ways to lead their organizations and achieve sustained success. And, because of these circumstances, there is a thirst for a pool of future leaders to be developed with the relevant next-generation leadership competencies and skills. This will enable them to seize the opportunities as well as manage the daunting challenges that have surfaced as a result of this new normal business environment (Hagemann and Bawany 2016).

The rapidly evolving demands of the 21st century include everything from climate change to demography, shifting customer requirements and expectations, rise of technology, globalization, new markets, and new attitudes toward work. Leaders must now operate in a way that inspires and engages employees while simultaneously addressing changing customer requirements and delivering results. Finally, all of these need to be achieved with a sense of urgency, as the experienced leaders of the Baby Boomer generation are retiring.

These diverse and escalating demands on leaders are reflected in the "2016 Trends in Executive Development: A Benchmark Report" published by the EDA. The wide-ranging and in-depth assessment is based on survey results from 466 organizations worldwide, with contributions from presidents, senior vice-presidents, chief learning officers, and heads of executive and leadership development (Hagemann and Bawany 2016).

It is evident that conventional leadership development practices are no longer adequate. Organizations globally need to incorporate the next-generation leadership competencies in order to address the development needs of their new leaders. This expanded group of upcoming leaders need to have a broader skillset, one that equips them to think and act globally in a VUCA business environment. They must do so while embracing cross-cultural diversity and cultivating collaborative relationships within and outside their walls. These are the hallmarks of the mindset needed to develop effective NextGen global leaders.

The next-generation leadership competencies will include the suite of cognitive readiness skills that can be viewed as part of the advanced thinking skills that make leaders ready to confront whatever new and complex problems they might face. Cognitive readiness is the mental preparation that leaders develop so that they, and their teams, are prepared to face the ongoing dynamic, ill-defined, and unpredictable challenges in the highly disruptive and VUCA-driven business environment. In the 2016 Trends in Executive Development: A Benchmark Report, the ability to create a vision and engage others is reported as the competency most lacking in next-generation leaders. This is consistent with the findings from past years' survey.

For details of the NextGen leadership competencies, please see Table 3.1 (Hagemann et al. 2016).

*Table 3.1 Competencies for the next generation of leaders*

| Top Five NextGen Leadership Competencies |
| --- |
| 1. Ability to create a vision and engage others around it |
| 2. Critical thinking |
| 3. Ability to attract, develop, and retain the quality of talent needed to achieve the business objectives |
| 4. Inspirational leadership: creating a vision, enrolling and empowering others |
| 5. Leading through change |

EDA has identified the following seven key cognitive readiness skills, collectively known as Paragon[7] (see Figure 3.3), which will develop, enhance, or sustain a leader's ability to navigate successfully in this new normal:

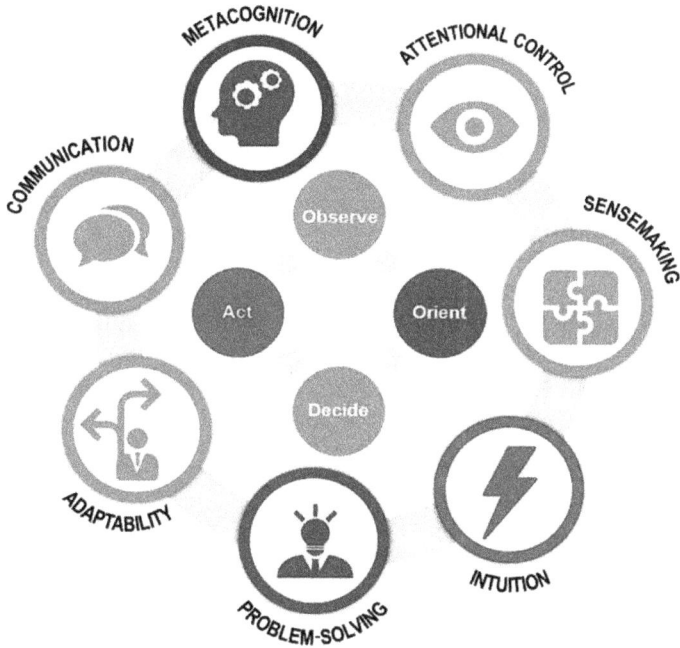

*Figure 3.3 Paragon[7] cognitive readiness competencies*

1. **Mental cognition:** Recognize and regulate your thoughts and emotions
2. **Attentional control:** Manage and focus your attention
3. **Sensemaking:** Connect the dots and see the bigger picture
4. **Intuition:** Check your gut, but don't let it rule your mind
5. **Problem-solving:** Use analytical and creative methods to resolve a challenge
6. **Adaptability:** Be willing and able to change, with shifting conditions
7. **Communication:** Inspire others to action; create fluid communication pathways

The detailed descriptors of each of these seven cognitive readiness competencies are shown in Table 3.2.

*Table 3.2 Descriptors of Paragon[7] cognitive readiness competencies*

| Metacognition | Attentional Control | Sensemaking |
|---|---|---|
| *Metacognition* is monitoring and managing your emotional and mental processes. Metacognition comes from the words "meta" meaning beyond and "cognition" meaning thinking. It describes the ability to control your mental and emotional processes and, in turn, manage behaviors and maximize performance. Metacognition involves self-awareness and the use of intentional strategies to self-regulate your cognition, emotions, and actions. Metacognitive individuals and organizations engage in reflective practice. They take time to plan before, during, and after situations. | *Attentional control* ("mindfulness") is the skill of actively managing your attention as a finite resource. Attentional control, or mindfulness, is the conscious control of your own attention. People or organizations with high levels of attentional control pick up on weak signals. They can direct and sustain their attention deliberately, without being diverted by distractions, and they can stay focused, even if that sustained attention becomes unpleasant. You can help develop your attentional control "muscles" by practicing attentional shifting and focusing exercises. | *Sensemaking* is the ability to quickly connect the dots to gain understanding. Sensemaking is pattern-based reasoning; in other words, it's the process of developing an understanding of an event or situation, particularly when it's complex and you lack clear, complete, and orderly data. Good sensemakers "put the pieces together" quickly and overcome information gaps. They discern meaning from patterns and recognize how parts of a system fit into the bigger picture, how individual elements interact, and how short-term goals impact long-term strategies. |

| Intuition | Problem-Solving | Adaptability | Communication |
|---|---|---|---|
| *Intuition* comes from your "fast thinking" (elephant) cognitive system. Intuition is fast; our minds quickly generate intuitive judgments without | *Problem-solving* is an analytical approach to resolving difficult issues. Problem-solving relies upon three factors: | *Adaptability* is the ability and willingness to change with shifting conditions. Adaptability is the consistent | *Communication* is about conveying deeper intent and understanding. Communication is the conveyance of information and sentiments. Clear, |

| Intuition | Problem-Solving | Adaptability | Communication |
|---|---|---|---|
| active deliberation. We all use intuition— especially under VUCA conditions— but our intuition isn't always reliable. It's important to know when it can be trusted and how to best use it. | subject-matter knowledge, motivation, and problem-solving "meta-skill," which is a mental list of problem-solving techniques and decision strategies typically associated with critical thinking and decision analysis tools. | willingness and ability to alter attitudes, thoughts, and behaviors to appropriately respond to actual or anticipated change in the environment. This includes flexibility, resilience, responsiveness, and agility. | honest, and frequent communication facilitates team performance. Beyond that, you can use linguistic tools to help increase saliency, clarity, relevance, and persuasive value. |

Overall, heightened cognitive readiness allows leaders to maintain a better sense of self-control in stressful situations.

## ESI Competencies

The next crucial NextGen leadership competency is that of ESI. Emotional intelligence (EI) has become a major topic of interest in organizations since the publication of a bestseller by the same name in 1995 by Daniel Goleman (1995). The early definitions of social intelligence influenced the way EI was later conceptualized. Contemporary theorists like Peter Salovey and John Mayer (1990) originally viewed EI as part of social intelligence, which suggests that both concepts are related and may, in all likelihood, represent interrelated components of the same construct.

Because individuals in organizations can rarely be successful alone, they must influence, lead, and coordinate their efforts with others in order to achieve their goals—to translate vision into action. A leader's success rests in large part upon the ability to influence and relate to the different groups in the organization: the superiors, peers, and direct reports.

In 1998, in *Working with Emotional Intelligence*, author Daniel Goleman set out a framework of EI that reflects how an individual's potential for mastering the skills of self-awareness, self-management, social awareness, and relationship management translates into on-the-job success for a leader. This model is based on EI competencies that have been identified in extensive published research on hundreds of corporations and organizations as distinguishing outstanding performers (Goleman 1998).

Emotional competence is defined as "a learned capability based on EI that results in outstanding performance at work" (Goleman 1988). To be adept at an emotional competence like customer service or conflict management requires an underlying ability in EI fundamentals, specifically social awareness and relationship management. However, emotional competencies are learned abilities: Having social awareness or skill at managing relationship does not guarantee we have mastered the additional learning required to handle a customer adeptly or to resolve a conflict—just that a leader has the potential to become skilled at these competencies.

Emotional competencies are job skills that can, and indeed must, be learned. An underlying EI ability is necessary, though not sufficient, to manifest competence in any one of the four EI domains or clusters (Goleman 2000). The competencies are classified into four clusters of general EI abilities:

1. **Self-awareness**
2. **Self-management**
3. **Social awareness**
4. **Relationship management**

Nested within each of those four areas are specific, learned competencies that set the best leaders and performers apart from the average (see Figure 3.4).

The framework illustrates, for example, that we cannot demonstrate the competencies of trustworthiness and conscientiousness without mastery of the fundamental ability of self-management, or the competencies

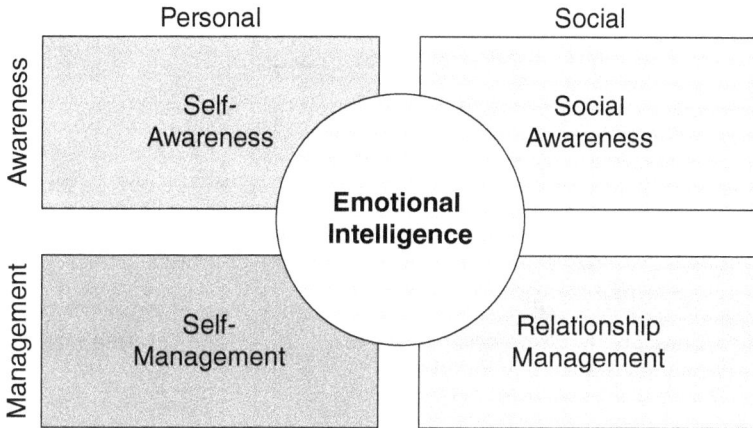

*Figure 3.4 The Goleman ESI framework*

of influence, communication, conflict management, without a handle on managing relationships.

**Self-awareness** concerns knowing one's internal states, preferences, resources, and intuitions. The self-awareness cluster contains three competencies:

A) Emotional self-awareness: recognizing one's emotions and their effects.
B) Accurate self-assessment: knowing one's strengths and limits.
C) Self-confidence: a strong sense of one's self-worth and capabilities.

**Self-management** refers to managing one's internal states, impulses, and resources. The self-management cluster contains six competencies:

A) Emotional self-control: keeping disruptive emotions and impulses in check.
B) Transparency: maintaining integrity, acting congruently with one's values.
C) Adaptability: flexibility in handling change.
D) Achievement: Striving to improve or meeting a standard of excellence.
E) Initiative: readiness to act on opportunities.
F) Optimism: persistence in pursuing goals despite obstacles and setbacks.

**Social awareness** refers to how people handle relationships and awareness of others' feelings, needs, and concerns. The social awareness cluster contains three competencies:

A) Empathy: sensing others' feelings and perspectives and taking an active interest in their concerns.
B) Organizational awareness: reading a group's emotional currents and power relationships.
C) Service orientation: anticipating, recognizing, and meeting customers' needs.

**Relationship management** concerns the skill or adeptness at inducing desirable responses in others. The relationship management cluster contains six competencies:

A) Developing others: sensing others' development needs and bolstering their abilities.
B) Inspirational leadership: inspiring and guiding individuals and groups.
C) Change catalyst: initiating or managing change.
D) Influence: wielding effective tactics for persuasion.
E) Conflict management: negotiating and resolving disagreements.
F) Teamwork and collaboration: working with others toward shared goals and creating group synergy in pursuing collective goals.

## Importance of Empathy as a Leadership Competency in Industry 4.0

In Industry 4.0, AI, robotics, and automation have gained a rapidly expanding foothold in the workplace, faster than many organizations ever expected. Leading companies are recognizing that these technologies are most effective when they complement humans and not replace them.

As these technologies permeate the workplace, cognitive readiness competencies such as critical thinking, creativity, problem-solving, and ESI gain in importance. One of the critical ESI skills that a leader needs to demonstrate in the workplace is empathy.

Empathy could be viewed as demonstrating the ability to sense others' feelings and how they see things as well as taking an active interest in their concerns. A leader picks up cues to what's being felt and thought by listening attentively to understand the other person's point of view, the terms in which they think about what's going on.

For example, in the health care industry, empathy and the jobs connected with it will be valued more and more in the future. It makes complete sense. Automation, robots, and AI will perform certain cognitive tasks brilliantly, to the extent that humans will not be able to compete. Where could humans have a chance? Although AI will perform diagnostic tasks or robots might be able to do surgeries, could they talk to a patient with empathy about the risks and consequences of an operation?

Moreover, as digital health simplifies administration and cuts down on monotonous tasks, the workload of doctors and nurses will be reduced, so they will be able to concentrate on what really matters—healing the patient and guiding them through the entire process with care. It is believed that, eventually, AI would be able to mimic even such soft skills but as we are social beings, we will always need the human touch.

Many leaders and managers vaguely understand the impact empathy has on leadership effectiveness. One of the reasons we have found is that very few of them have been trained or taught how to cultivate empathy in their lives and work as a daily practice (Bawany 2017). The empathetic leader puts themselves in their followers' shoes and attempts to see things from their perspective. Empathy doesn't mean agreeing with someone. Empathy is not sympathy. Empathy doesn't mean telling them that they are right or even addressing their concern. Demonstrating empathy shows that you care enough to give someone else's issue the same level of respect and attention they do.

Empathy can be simply defined as the ability to be aware of and understand how others feel. It is a key component of people-oriented and participative leadership. This would include being sensitive to the feelings, concerns, and needs of the coworkers, and the ability to see the world from their perspective.

Empathy can also be seen as demonstrating an active concern for people and their needs by forming close and supportive relationships with others. Leaders who lack empathy may be perceived by others as cold, uncaring, and having little interest in them as people. Leaders who score high on this competency work to develop close bonds with others. They spend time getting to know people and are able to give their colleagues the feeling that they are personally involved with them. They tend to emphasize the importance of being generous and kind and displaying a sincere interest in the well-being of others. If carried to extremes, however, this closeness may cloud a leader's objectivity and result in decisions that do not properly consider the organization's best interests. Hence, it would be crucial for the leader to bear in mind the saying, "familiarity breeds contempt."

Organizations need to incorporate a different form of development activities for their next generation of leaders, which are likely to include executive coaching, mentoring, personal development, and stretch assignments. Other development activities include psychometric assessments, managerial coaching, performance feedback, and customized training programs developed by internal staff. All of these activities have strong developmental value as components of an overall executive leadership development strategy. In addition, the organization needs to ensure that these leaders are also equipped with cognitive readiness skills and ESI competencies needed for sustained success and effectiveness in a VUCA environment.

## "LEAP" Framework for Leading through the Fog in a VUCA-Driven Industry 4.0

To lead and manage the managerial challenges successfully in the VUCA-driven Industry 4.0, leaders need to "LEAP" through the fog (Bawany 2016) and demonstrate the cognitive readiness competencies as explained in the earlier section and at the same time possess the traits depicted in Figure 3.5, which are defined as follows:

Liberal: open to developing new behavior, skills, or opinions and willing to adapt or discard existing values if and when necessary to adapt to the *new normal.*

Exuberant: filled with lively energy with a sense of passion and optimism (while grounded to reality) in engaging the team and other stakeholders.

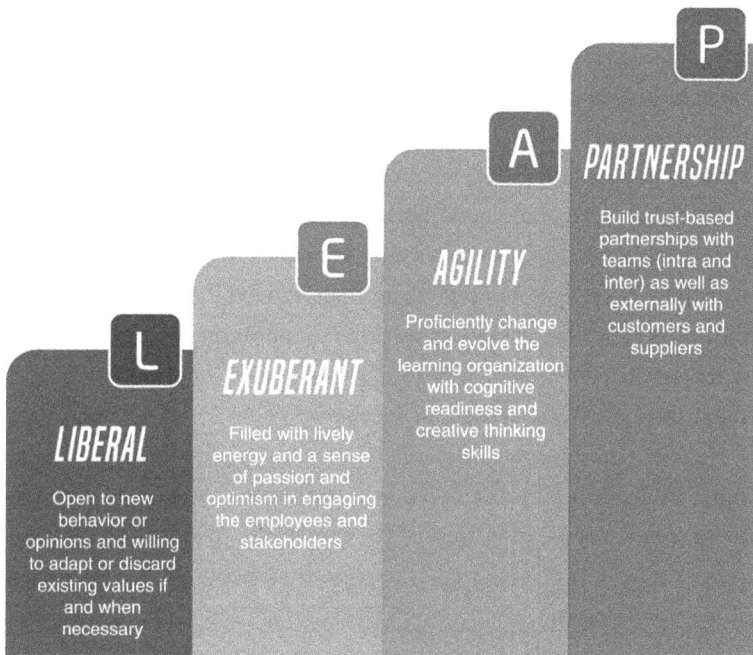

*Figure 3.5  The "LEAP" framework of leading in Industry 4.0*

**Agility:** proficiently manage change with resilience and demonstrate learning and mental agility within a learning organization with NextGen leadership competencies, including cognitive readiness, critical thinking, and ESI.

**Partnership:** build a trust-based partnership with teams (by removing silos) as well as externally with other stakeholders, including customers and suppliers.

## Microsoft Corporation: Case Study of Leadership in the Development of HPOs

In today's hypercompetitive, disruptive VUCA-driven business environment, we need a new breed of CEOs and business leaders who are defined less by commanding and controlling or autocratic/coercive and pacesetting leadership styles and more by inspiring and empowering, or authoritative/visionary and coaching leadership styles (Bawany 2017).

A good example of a leader who demonstrates this approach effectively and successfully is Microsoft Corporation CEO Satya Nadella. Unlike his predecessor, the notoriously combative Steve Ballmer, Nadella has dramatically revived Microsoft's reputation and its relevance by emphasizing collaboration and what he calls a "learn-it-all" culture versus the company's historical know-it-all one. As *Fast Company*'s senior editor Harry McCracken (2017) explains in "Microsoft Rewrites the Code," the results have been eye-popping: more than $250 billion in market value gains in less than four years—a feat that, quantitatively, puts Nadella in the league of Jeff Bezos of Amazon, Tim Cook of Apple, Larry Page of Google, and Mark Zuckerberg of Facebook.

Nadella demonstrates ontological humility: A few months into his tenure, he made a major faux pas at a conference for women engineers that spawned a wave of criticism. He owned the mistake and admitted to biases that he hadn't realized. The episode ended up building his credibility in the long run.

Nadella's leadership style is to emphasize what's been done right. He starts each senior leadership meeting with a segment called "Researcher of the Amazing," showcasing something inspiring at the company, and, by doing so, he created an organizational climate of trust partnership with his coleaders.

Nadella is a strong believer in talent management and has been personally involved in the recruitment of new talent into the company. He has emphasized the importance of an outsider's perspective in steering the organization to greater heights. He has put even more focus on unleashing potential within the leadership team, including high-potential leaders. He has created a high-performance-driven culture with his empowering and coaching style of leadership, which relies on managerial coaching as an organizational development tool. He also believes that resistance to change is a behavior rather than a fixed personality trait and that it can be addressed with coaching.

Finally, Nadella demonstrates empathy as he recognizes that his coleaders' and employees' perspectives are real and important to them. It may not be real, or important, to him, but it is very real and important to them. He gives it the same level of respect and attention they do.

# Conclusion

HPOs exhibit a set of characteristics that are available to almost every company, regardless of the industry and scale of business. However, to achieve sustainable success, companies may benefit from the experience of those that have achieved it. It could be helpful if they are able to examine and benchmark every aspect of the business, including strategy, structure, people, climate, and processes, and take steps to bring their organizations in line with the high-performance profile.

Leading an HPO in a highly disruptive and increasingly VUCA-driven business environment and workplace requires leaders to leverage on their cognitive readiness skills and relationship management skills. This will enable the leader to connect emotionally with the team members so as to understand them better and ensure they always feel confident in what they are doing. The leader does not just feel for their people, they feel with them.

# CHAPTER 4

# Identifying, Assessing, and Selecting NextGen Leaders

## Introduction

Today's dramatically changing work environment demands that organizations need to continuously ensure that there is a robust leadership pipeline ready to be deployed now and in the future. Identifying, assessing, selecting, and developing the next-generation or potential future leaders are, therefore, critical strategic objectives for ensuring a sustainable, competitive organization.

The business case for doing so is clear as supported by extensive research. In the first 18 months of ascending to leadership positions, 30 to 70 percent of leaders fail (Hogan 2011). These failures cost organizations substantial time and resources, with estimates ranging from $750,000 to over $2.5 million to replace senior leaders. The estimated cost of replacing a CEO is an astounding $12 million to $52 million (Stoddard and Wyckoff 2009). Equally important, indirect costs are associated with leader failure, including increased employee stress and decreased engagement (Schippmann 2010).

Hence, organizations need to augment their leadership bench strength and also ensure the availability of leaders today and tomorrow to take on the responsibility to ensure the sustainability of the organization. In essence, the heart of the leadership challenge that confronts today's leaders is also applicable to the next generation of leaders who will be expected to lead.

One of the challenges of identifying high-potential individuals is the inherent complexity of making predictions about how successful a person might be in the long-term future. It involves defining what you are trying to predict, assessing a person against the appropriate criteria, and making predictions about future performance. A wide range of issues need to be considered, including the person's capabilities and motivations, and the challenges and opportunities associated with future positions in the organization. This is different from a selection decision where there is a clear understanding of the specific job requirements for the position to be filled.

## NextGen Leadership Pipeline

Leading organizations continuously ask themselves where their future or next-generation leaders will come from. It would seem that the same approach has been implemented for a long time. This includes identifying high-potential talents within the workforce, providing them with development opportunities, and equipping them with critical skills and competencies required to drive the organization strategy (Bawany 2014c). Given the daunting challenges that these future leaders will face in the highly disruptive and volatile, uncertain, complex, and ambiguous (VUCA)–driven business environment, there is a need for organizations to continuously reassess their approach toward ensuring the development of the right set of skills and competencies for their NextGen leaders (Bawany 2017).

One of the most important, yet misunderstood, questions within talent management is how to successfully identify and manage high-potential employees—those talented few who can and will step up and deliver in bigger, broader roles. Smart businesses know how to take full advantage of their talent by identifying those who have the highest potential. This ability to identify the elusive "potential" in an employee is considered a key competitive advantage (Silzer and Dowell 2010).

According to the Corporate Leadership Council (2010), most companies believe that their high-potential employees are more than 50 percent valuable than an average employee. Not surprisingly, over three-quarters of these companies indicate that high-potential identification is an immediate short-term priority. The investment in high potentials has also increased, with 80 percent of companies claiming to have spent more dollars than before on this group. The appeal of these companies is clear on the other side as well—promising talent is attracted to companies known for having strong development resources and opportunities (Fernández-Aráoz, Groysberg, and Nohria 2011).

Talent management represents an organization's efforts to attract, develop, and retain skilled and valuable employees. Its goal is to have people with the capabilities and commitment needed for current and future organizational success. An organization's talent pool, particularly its managerial talent, is often referred to as the leadership pipeline (Conger and Fulmer 2003). Developing the next generation of leaders involves building a sustainable leadership pipeline for the organization.

Ram Charan introduced the image of a leadership "pipeline" (see Figure 4.1) and asserts that, if whatever is flowing through it gets stuck, the pipeline will not deliver the resource it contains (Charan, Drotter, and Noel 2001). Where the pipeline shifts direction, things can easily get stuck. It is the task of managers who lead to help those who get stuck to move on (up or out) and make room for others.

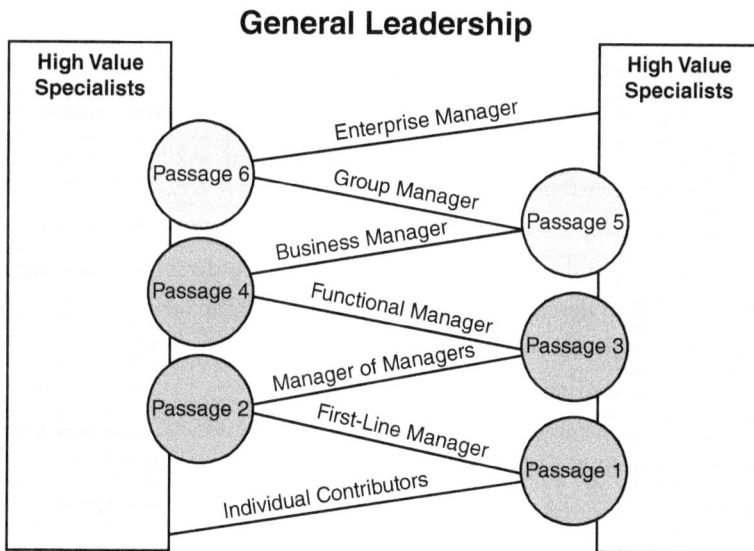

**General Leadership**

High Value Specialists

High Value Specialists

Enterprise Manager

Passage 6

Group Manager

Passage 5

Business Manager

Passage 4

Functional Manager

Passage 3

Manager of Managers

Passage 2

First-Line Manager

Passage 1

Individual Contributors

Figure 4.1 The leadership pipeline framework

## The Business Case for Developing the Leadership Pipeline

As explained in Chapter 2, NextGen leaders are primarily the high potentials of the organization. High-potential talent is often viewed as an employee who is assessed as having the ability, commitment, and align-ment to the organization's values and has demonstrated the competen-cies and skills as well as the motivation to rise to and succeed in more senior positions in the organization. Each organization will have their own definitions of high-potential talent, but in essence, the process and criteria for assessment and identification of high potentials are quite similar.

A robust leadership pipeline is critical to driving strategy and growth so that organizations can achieve their goals. It can contribute to a sus-tainable competitive advantage for the organization. While many or-ganizations have devoted considerable resources to the development of future leaders, few have an available pool of these leaders who are ready to take on greater responsibilities and to meet the daunting challenges of the future. This remains one of the critical talent management issues facing organizations operating in a VUCA business environment around the world.

While the severity of the issue varies among organizations and indus-tries, it is clear throughout the business world that the demand for these future leaders is greater than the supply. The complexity and fast-changing nature of the hypercompetitive global economy have created the demand for new leadership mindsets, skills, and capabilities. As a result, many or-ganizations face a shortage of leadership talent. If leadership development programs fail to develop people fast enough to fill the new and changing roles required for success, it will put organizations in a predicament, and their long-term sustainability is in question.

Developing a leadership pipeline starts with identifying and then transforming high-potential individuals through a variety of develop-mental opportunities and experiences (Bawany 2014a). This is achieved by identifying and cultivating emerging talent early on while enhanc-ing organizational capability. But organizations face unprecedented chal-lenges in their effort to cultivate new leadership. This includes developing leaders from different generations (likely to be from Gen Y or millennials), meeting the demand for leaders with global fluency and flexibility, having the ability to innovate and inspire others to perform, and acquiring new levels of understanding of rapidly changing and emerging technologies and new disciplines and fields.

As experienced leaders, managers, and professionals continue to leave an organization, their intellectual capital and tacit knowledge, unless codified, will be lost. This adds to the challenges, especially at a time when the market is growing globally. It also translates to tougher competition in the marketplace, making the search for high-potential people more difficult and future success more elusive. Furthermore, there is a sense of urgency for organizations today to accelerate the effort to build competence, and this compounds the challenge of building a strong leadership pipeline from within (Bawany 2018d).

## Identification and Assessment of NextGen Leaders (High Potentials)

In recent years, the use of formal assessment efforts has broadened both within and across organizations (Scott and Reynolds 2010). The increasing emphasis on the hunt and competition for talent, first identified in the early 2000s (Michaels, Handfield-Jones, and Axelrod 2001), has raised awareness levels and concern over an organization's ability to fill gaps in the leadership pipeline. This, in turn, has led to an increasing emphasis and focus on talent management strategies and frameworks in organizations (Cappelli 2008), including the creation of new job titles, dedicated roles, and entire functions dedicated to this area of focus.

It has also led to a heightened focus on high-potential identification in corporations (e.g., Campbell and Smith 2010). In particular, there is an increasing emphasis on finding the most effective assessment method or tool that will identify future leaders with the greatest potential for enhanced development and succession. The leadership development training programs may be strengthened, broadened, and deepened to enhance the capability to inspire and engage others as well as cognitive readiness skills and emotional and social intelligence competencies. These capabilities can be addressed by incorporating specific activities and exercises designed to increase awareness of their impact and importance through using familiar techniques such as case studies or applicable business simulation models.

In addition, opportunities for application and practice can be provided in experience-based approaches where participants work to apply the concepts and skills directly to real business issues, while colleagues and facilitators provide feedback on the basis of behaviors they observed during their work together.

Many organizations recognize that assessment, selection, and development procedures for their people are of paramount importance to achieve a sustainable competitive advantage. Increasingly, they are turning to the *Assessment Center* (AC) approach, which, when carefully constructed and well run, can provide a number of benefits to an organization seeking to improve its approach to the selection and development of their talent. This can, in turn, identify and predict key behaviors in the workplace that can transform future leaders. These benefits may include, but are not limited to, the following:

1. Reduction in turnover and subsequent recruitment costs (as the most appropriate individual is selected for the leadership role)
2. Identification of high-potential talent within an organization
3. Identification of individual strengths
4. Identification of individual development needs
5. Identification of crucial "skills gaps" to drive the organization forward
6. Provision of a robust process for the restructuring of the organization if needed
7. Provision of relevant and credible information for succession planning
8. Execution of a detailed talent audit within the whole organization

The purpose of an AC is to obtain the best possible indication of a person's actual or potential capability to perform in the target job or level of responsibility. The AC is designed to focus on the systematic and objective identification of behaviors of an individual for the purposes of selection, placement, promotion, development, career management, succession planning, and training. The AC method is now regarded as one of the most accurate and valid assessment procedures and is used globally for both selection and development.

## Leveraging on an AC

It is difficult to provide an exact definition of an AC because its content may differ widely depending on the objectives of the program for each organization. In general, however, an AC involves the standardized evaluation of behaviors, and the following key factors should be included in the process:

1. **Assessments are behavioral based:** The primary purpose of an AC is the evaluation of the performance of participants against a preidentified set of competencies or criteria. These competencies or criteria can be identified by carrying out a thorough job analysis of the role in question (whether the job is an existing one or a new position). These criteria should incorporate the participant's knowledge, ability, personality, and personal motivation. This will enable the identification of those behaviors that differentiate successful from the less successful performance. It is also important at this stage to ensure that the context in which the behaviors take place is understood, together with the level of complexity of the problems likely to be encountered by the jobholder.

2. **Several candidates or participants are observed together:** This allows interaction between participants, both in the actual exercises and less formally, ensuring that the program is more interactive as well as more economical. With the increasing advances in technology, these groups can be formed not only physically but also in the form of, for example, a virtual AC. While there are no hard-and-fast rules on the number of participants to be involved in each center, the practical considerations for the design of the center usually require multiples of four or six participants.

3. **Assessment is via a combination of methods:** A key factor in the design of a center is the inclusion of at least two work sample simulations that replicate, as far as possible, the key challenges of the job in question. These simulation exercises will typically be used in combination with other assessment techniques to ensure comprehensive coverage of attributes and skills and to increase the reliability of measurement. Two important factors to bear in mind when selecting appropriate assessment methods are:
   i) Do they capture the different situational contexts of the job?
   ii) Do they provide the opportunity for the accurate assessment of the range of skills and competencies required to perform the job?

When designing the AC program and selecting the assessment methods to use, it is important to ensure that there are at least two measures for every competency to be assessed.

4. **Multiple assessors or observers:** The involvement of a number of assessors increases both objectivity and impartiality. A key factor in the use of multiple assessors is that the timetable should be designed in such a way as to allow for their rotation so that, ideally, a range of assessors observe each participant. The assessors can be taken from a range of personnel specialists, line managers, and psychologists. All should be fully trained in the behavioral assessment process and in its application to the particular exercises being used in the center.

5. **Integration of data:** An integration session provides a fair and objective review of all the evidence gathered and aims to gain consensus among the assessors. The aim is to focus on the participant's overall performance against the competency model and to identify a pattern or profile of strengths and development needs of each individual. When used for selection, no decision should be taken until all the evidence has been shared and a final rating agreed upon. This session should be used to gather information to provide feedback to the participant on their strengths and potential development areas, and the participant may even be given some feedback during the AC. Ideally, no one assessor should have all the data on a single participant until the integration session.

### Lessons Learned from Derailment of High-Potential Identification

It would be prudent to learn from mistakes that organizations have made in identifying candidates that were eventually proven not to succeed in future leadership roles. Interestingly, most managers will nominate high performers (based on past performance), but the selection is not validated with some form of observational or psychometric assessment or through an AC. These managers mistakenly assume that high performers are automatically high potentials (Bawany 2018d).

There are research findings that clearly support the case; these seem to point to the fact that only 20 percent or less of high-performing employees are also high potentials (Ready, Conger, and Hill 2010). A manager may be a high performer at their current level but struggle with a higher-level business leadership role due to increased demands and capabilities required to succeed in those roles. Furthermore, after implementing a high-potential identification program in the company, there are no organizational systems or processes to develop, rotate, or deploy candidates to help them gain the right experience so that they can prepare themselves for their next role.

Leading organizations develop their high-potential leaders best through job-based exposure and stretch experiences, so the organization must have a well-defined process to support these activities. For those high-potential leaders who are not managed under a structured development process, many or most lose faith in the company's desire to provide for their career and may leave the company to pursue their career goals with another firm. On the other hand, there are many instances that many or most of these high potentials stay with their current companies when they can see that their future is aligned with the company's future.

Often managers and executives confuse assessing an individual's current skills and abilities with that individual's potential, just as they confuse past performance with future effectiveness. Current skills and abilities are different from potential and need to be considered separately. Accurately assessing a person's current knowledge, skills, and abilities is an important first step, but it should not be confused with determining the person's ability to grow, adapt, and develop enough to handle more complex future work challenges and responsibilities. Unfortunately, this difference is not typically recognized or discussed in most organizations, even when they understand the difference between past performance and future effectiveness. This may be due to not only a poor understanding of the difference but also a poor definition and measurement of potential.

Unfortunately, the judgment about an employee's future potential is often left to a hasty discussion at the end of a long succession planning meeting, and the decision is frequently made by few or even a single senior executive. Few organizations have specifically defined what they mean by potential or how an individual employee's potential differs from their past performance or their current abilities and skills. Even when potential is clearly defined, the judgment can be difficult. How do you evaluate a person's ability to grow and develop in the future? Making predictions about the future is more complex than assessing a person's current skills and abilities. It may be similar to predicting progress on other development variables (Silzer and Church 2010).

In 2009, Executive Development Associates (EDA) embarked on a research and published the findings of its study on the identification of high-potential leadership talent. The respondents were asked to address the factors they consider important to identify high-potential leadership talent (Hagemann and Bolt 2009). The following factors as listed in Table 4.1 are rated the highest:

*Table 4.1 Factors in identifying of high potentials*

| Factors Important for the Identification of High-Potential Talent | Explanation/Description |
| --- | --- |
| Strong track record of performance, proven results, and success in past or current roles | Executives said they look at how successfully candidates perform their various job duties individually and compared with their peers. For instance, one executive said she looks for successful people in their current roles; another looks at job performance, and a third stressed standing out above the rest. One executive asked, "What kind of results are they getting? Did they go beyond what was initially laid out, and did they complete the project?" |
| Strong interpersonal skills | Understanding the people side of business. Interpersonal skills were described as softer skills and included the ability to interact with diverse individuals; to recognize how actions will affect themselves, others, and the business; to understand the people side of the business and to express empathy. When describing individuals who have strong interpersonal skills, one executive said he looked for people who are not all about themselves. One executive asked himself, "How do they achieve results? How do they work with people to get the work done?" |
| Strong communication skills | Strong communication skills include excellent verbal and written communication. Excellent verbal and written communication and clear, concise communication at all levels were emphasized repeatedly as key predictors of future success. One executive identified high potentials by their ability to give presentations and how well they communicate and handle conflict. For many, the ability to communicate with their team was critical. |

| Factors Important for the Identification of High-Potential Talent | Explanation/Description |
|---|---|
| Drive, initiative, or ambition to accept an increased level of responsibility or the willingness to readily accept new challenges | High potentials were described as hungry individuals who are self-driven and do not expect the company to take them in any certain direction. Always thinking of a better "mousetrap," these individuals are spotted by their initiative, persistence, drive, and, importantly, their work ethic. One executive searches for individuals who are always dissatisfied with the status quo—looking to change what needs changing. One of the role-model leaders asked himself, "Does the individual have an interest and desire to learn more and to take on more responsibilities?" |
| An ability to create and articulate company vision and strategy; set direction, execute objectives, and understand the total business | Not only is it important to understand the company vision and strategy, it is also important to look for individuals who are vision-setters, meaning they have a vision, share that vision, execute that vision, and get others to buy into that vision. In other words, they create a vision for people to follow. One of the executives mentioned that high potentials should have no fear of personalizing the strategy and vision or of seeking input from subordinates because that is often what it takes to understand the dynamics across the organization and to have a clear point of view in understanding the (total) business and its context. |

## Competency-Based Selection of NextGen Leaders (High Potentials)

The work of David McClelland (1973) set the stage for the widespread growth of competencies. McClelland argued that aptitude tests, almost universally used to predict performance, do not serve their intended purpose well and are prone to cultural biases. Also, he argued that other traditional measures, such as examination results and references, are equally poor at predicting job success. Instead, McClelland suggested that individual competence might provide a more promising alternative for predicting performance. He described competencies as representing groups of behaviors underlying individual characteristics that enable superior job performance.

The 1980s witnessed growth in using competencies to identify and predict leadership effectiveness and long-term success (Boyatzis 1982; McClelland and Boyatzis 1982). These applications led to the development of leadership competency models and competency-based selection tools, such as behavioral event interviews (Boyatzis 1994; McClelland 1998). Competencies also provide a structure for linking performance with cognitive ability and personality, coaching employees to overcome dysfunctional behavior (Boyatzis 2006), and selecting and developing high-potential employees (McClelland 1994).

Managers are required to ensure that organizations achieve their objectives. Managerial competencies are defined as sets of knowledge, skills, behaviors, and attitudes that a person needs in order to be effective in a wide range of managerial jobs and various types of organizations. Organizations applying several managerial competencies, which draws attention to the need to understand how different these competencies are working in organizations, therefore, are required to highlight the most effective competency in order to enhance it for a good performance.

Competency is an important concept in organization management since it is closely related to excellent work performance. Individual competencies are one of the factors that determine the effectiveness of organizational performance. Managerial competency models located in the literature capture business skills, intra- and interpersonal skills, and leadership skills as important competencies for effective performance. Managerial competence is the ability of managers and leaders to direct work streams and define outcomes clearly. Identifying the requisite competencies for achieving in an occupational field is a critical process in management, where the task of identifying qualities defines the efficiency of managers. Competency often means "a fairly deep and enduring part of a person's personality" (Levenson 2011).

Competent managers have been required by the organizations from the early 1950s (Boyatzis 1982). Managers are required to ensure that organizations achieve their objectives. Many researchers over a period of time have tried to identify and establish competencies that are required for managerial effectiveness leading to superior performance. Managers may thus be seen as seeking to give, take, and manage knowledge through work and the organization. Boyatzis (1982) defines managerial competencies as characteristics that are causally related to effective and/or superior job performance. Boyatzis (2008) also analyzed managerial competencies and defined competencies as an underlying characteristic of a person that could be a motive, trait, skill, aspect of one's self-image, social role, or a body of knowledge that they use. These characteristics are revealed in observable and identifiable patterns of behavior, related to job performance and usually include knowledge, skill, and abilities.

Earlier in Chapter 3, we have discussed the specific competencies that NextGen leaders need to demonstrate to succeed in today's "new normal," which includes cognitive readiness, critical thinking, and emotional and social intelligence.

Leadership competencies are the most frequently assessed criteria for high potentials and future leaders. Competencies have become fully embedded in the language and practice of leadership assessment, selection, and development, and they also help drive business strategy, but they are not the only way to measure leadership effectiveness.

Some organizations believe that competencies are not the most appropriate target for leadership assessments and that organizations would be better served to define leadership effectiveness on the basis of expected outcomes rather than on proficiency in a set of competencies. People with many different styles and skills can achieve excellence in leadership; therefore, organizations should select and develop leaders for their overall competence and not just based on a list of attributes (Hollenbeck and McCall 2001).

Morgan W. McCall of the University of Southern California has defined a set of five leadership demands that can serve as the basis for evaluating leadership competence (see Table 4.2). These leadership

*Table 4.2 McCall's five leadership demands*

| Set and communicate direction | Establish and communicate the purpose, vision, and mission of your part of the organization. Create architecture and set of processes that will drive that vision. |
|---|---|
| Align critical constituencies | Make sure that the people and groups necessary to achieve the mission understand it and are aligned with it and that those who are obstacles to the mission are dealt with. |
| Demonstrate an executive temperament | Show the ability and confidence necessary to cope effectively with the pressures and ambiguity of a leadership role. |
| Set and live your values | Convey and reinforce what the organization—and you as a leader and person—believe in and stand for. |
| Grow and learn | Take the necessary steps to ensure that you and your people continue to learn, grow, and change. |

demands are drawn from successful leaders and reflect hundreds of descriptions of experiences and thousands of lessons learned (McCall 2010). Assessing a leader on the basis of how well he or she meets these five demands avoids the search for a single style, personality, or set of competencies common to all leaders.

The field of identifying and assessing high-potential talent in organizations is evolving. On the basis of challenges identified through various research reports discussed in the earlier sections of this chapter, we believe several key issues in the area are needed to be addressed in the future in order to advance the field.

There is certainly room to do better in terms of identifying high potentials. The greatest opportunity for improvement starts with having a clear definition of potential, followed by a systematic assessment of those nominated for inclusion in the high-potential pool. Increasingly, leading companies use the competency-based talent review process to select and align on high potentials.

# CHAPTER 5

# Development and Coaching of NextGen Leaders

## Introduction

Talent management represents an organization's efforts to attract, develop, and retain skilled and valuable employees. Its goal is to have people with the capabilities and commitment needed for current and future organizational success. An organization's talent pool, particularly its managerial talent, is often referred to as the leadership pipeline (Charan et al. 2000). However, one of the biggest challenges facing organizations today is that they are under greater pressure to develop future or next-generation leaders faster in response to the challenges ahead for business and HR leaders in a dramatically changing digital, volatile, uncertain, complex, and ambiguous (VUCA) business landscape (Bawany 2018f).

The high impact and cost of a new leader derailing within the first year are staggering. As Michael Watkins (2003) states in his book *The First 90 Days*, "studies have found that more than 40 to 50 percent of senior outside hires fail to achieve results" (p. 8). The reason for most of these failures is primarily not lack of intelligence (IQ), emotional and social intelligence skills (EQ), or experience; rather, it is the inability of these executives to assimilate themselves effectively into the new culture or new role and make the necessary "mindset shift" as they go through fundamental changes in roles.

Developing future leaders requires alignment between the achievement of business goals and leaders' skills to drive the achievement of those goals. To accomplish this, the organization needs to start with the creation of a business strategy, followed by a leadership strategy, and later a leadership development strategy. It is important to know the distinctions:

**Business strategy:** the roadmap for achieving the organization's business goals.

**Leadership strategy:** the organization's plan for assigning leaders in key job roles by defining the relevant competencies, including skills, knowledge, and experiences required to achieve the organization's desired current and future business goals.

**Leadership development strategy:** the organization's plan for the development of current and future leaders at all levels to ensure that they, individually and collectively, have the crucial and relevant competencies and skills to lead and drive the organization's strategy successfully now and in the future.

## The Background of Executive Coaching as a Developmental Tool

The history of coaching can be traced back as far as to Socrates (427 BC-347 BC). Socrates suggested that people learn best when they take personal responsibility and ownership of a given situation (Edwards 2003). The word "coach," however, originates from "Kocs," a village in Hungary, where high-quality carriages were produced. In the 19th century, English university students began to use this word as slang for tutors that helped them through their academic career. They said they were in a carriage driven by their tutor (Wilson 2004).

Coaching first appeared in management literature in the 1950s. Managers began using coaching since it was understood that a manager had a responsibility to improve subordinates' performance through a sort of master–apprentice relationship. Coaching, at that time, often took the form of the manager coaching the employees. In the mid-1970s, a sport coaching was starting to make its way and being translated into the managerial situation. Since the 1980s, coaching has been presented as a training technique in the context of management development. Coaching literature nowadays makes a connection with mentoring, career development, management development over a long period of time, and generating team and individual performance (Evered and Selman 1989).

Athletes and actors have known the value of coaching for many years (King and Eaton 1999). As O'Shaughnessy (2001) expressed, "as anyone who has watched a superbly-fought tennis match will testify, it is often down to how the contestants play a couple of crucial points" (p. 194). One might even say minimal differences in performance are of crucial importance in defining how someone's career will plan out.

In today's competitive world, no athlete should assume that it is possible to make it to the top without world-class coaching support (Burdett 1998). Mike Powell, a 32-year-old American long jump champion, gave credit for his achievements in the long jump event to a five-year scientific training plan designed by his coach Randy Huntington (Liu et al. 1998).

It is suggested that what is true in sports in general is also true in business (O'Shaughnessy 2001). In sports as well as in more conventional organizational models, individual excellence and teamwork are equally important. Teamwork is just as important as individual excellence since it is the ability to move beyond one's ego, showing a willingness to put the needs of the organization above personal gain, and a desire to win.

Today, business takes place in a highly competitive international arena, and the only way for companies to become successful is to push themselves to the very edge of their capability. There is only so much an organization can do productively in regard to downsizing, restructuring, focusing on the core business, and so on; ultimately, the success of the organization depends on the people within it—building a winning team. As a result, coaching has become a secret weapon for many organizations (Burdett 1998).

According to Parsloe and Wray (2000), coaching can be defined as follows:

> Coaching is a process that enables learning and development to occur and thus performance to improve. To be a successful coach requires knowledge and understanding of the process as the variety of styles, skills, and techniques that are appropriate to the context in which the coaching takes place. (p. 41)

## The Differences between Coaching, Managing, Consulting, and Training

Coaching, managing, consulting, and training are all related, and sometimes overlap. However, at their foundation, they are distinct in their focus.

A professional coach's primary attention is to tap into the client's own vision, wisdom, and directed action in service of the client's self-identified agenda. The client applies himself/herself to his/her whole life usually including, and often focusing on, their professional endeavors.

A manager's primary attention is to achieve specific organizational results through their direct reports. To that end, they may direct and/or develop those direct reports through performance feedback and may use coaching skills.

A consultant's primary attention is to achieve organizational results (often large systems change) through the application of specific expertise. They may or may not also be charged with transferring knowledge or skill sets to their client.

A training and development professional's primary attention is to the successful transfer of specific information or skills to their clients. Again, a trainer may well use a coactive approach and coaching skills.

## Leveraging on Executive Coaching for the Development of NextGen Leaders

Executive coaching is a concept that has moved from the world of sports to the executive suite and is designed as a means to help senior executives manage a constantly changing business environment and refine their leadership skills. But coaching is not limited to senior levels. Increasingly, people all over the world, at all levels, utilize executive coaches to help them achieve their full potential. The process focuses on the participant's goals, reinforces learning and change, and increases self-empowerment (Bawany, 2014d).

Executive coaching is one of the fastest growing and most misunderstood professions of this decade. Coaching used to be an "executive perk" for large company executives to help them make better business decisions. Today, coaching is rapidly being recognized as one of the best strategic weapons a company can have in its arsenal.

Executive coaching focuses on developing a top executive's full potential by coaching them to think and act beyond existing limits and paradigms. Executive coaching is a highly individualized form of leadership development and support available. It is based on the understanding that in order to be maximally effective, executives must accurately identify their strengths and areas of development, examine the impact of their behavior on others, and regularly and intentionally reflect on their values, goals, and effectiveness.

The strength of executive coaching lies in the fact that it is almost exclusively an executive development strategy that builds leadership and management strength because it is ultimately concerned with understanding where the executive is, where they want to go, and the things that they would have to do to get there. It is often lonely at the top for chief executives as they generally keep their own counsel, mainly because they find it difficult to discuss matters with colleagues and cannot or choose not to share their concerns with spouses and families. Executive coaching offers a way out of this by providing an opportunity for the executive to have an independent sounding board and strategic partner in a safe and confidential environment.

Executive coaching can be defined as a confidential, highly personal learning process, involving action learning and working in partnership, combining an executive coach's observations and capabilities with an executive's expertise. The result is that the executive achieves better and faster results-oriented outcomes. It is therefore important to create a coaching environment that is founded on trust because, in a normal working day, the executive works in a fast-paced, complex, and pressured environment, and there is little time to sit back and reflect on the range of issues facing them.

Savvy organizations acknowledge that executive coaching is a proven effective leadership intervention tool of choice for the next generation of leaders, including high potentials, for the continuous development of their leadership skills is critical to organization-wide success.

A study by Manchester, Inc. examined the impact of coaching in 56 companies with 100 executives (Manchester Inc. 2001). Their findings suggest that 74 percent of the sponsors and 86 percent of the participants were very satisfied with the process. From the survey of respondents who received coaching, it was estimated that coaching resulted in an average return of 5.7 times the initial investment. Furthermore, coaching contributed to a perception of increased productivity for 53 percent of respondents and improved quality of work for 48 percent of the respondents. When asked which workgroup relationships improved as a result of coaching, the results indicated that 77 percent reported improvement with direct reports, 71 percent reported improvement with immediate supervisors, and 63 percent reported improvement with peers. Of those receiving coaching, 61 percent reported a significant increase in their overall level of work and job satisfaction.

Executive coaching is typically seen as an ongoing relationship with no set time frame or definitive ending point. For example, the leader may have poor communication skills and is unintentionally undermining direct reports, which can lead to a loss of morale and retention issues. In corrective situations, the executive coach begins by completing a full diagnosis of the situation through the identification of undesirable behaviors, such as berating or blaming others, and demonstrates the consequences these behaviors will have on the individual and the organization. The coach then helps the executive identify practical ways to strengthen their leadership impact, provides direct and objective feedback, and ensures the executive gets back on track and stays on track.

Whether the relationship starts with a derailment situation or as part of a corporate-wide initiative, executive coaching covers a wide range of situations with one common goal: the personal development of a leader through the support of a professional relationship. On the organizational level, executive coaches help companies avoid costly management turnover, develop their most talented people, and ensure that leaders perform at their maximum potential. In research published in the *Industrial and Commercial Training*, it was reported that executives who received coaching are more likely to be promoted or to receive accelerated promotions than those who have not had one-on-one coaching (Parker-Wilkins 2006).

## Executive Coaching versus Transition Coaching

Effective coaching is a major key to improving business performance. Executive coaching focuses on the qualities of effective leadership and improved business results. It comprises a series of structured, one-on-one interactions between a coach and an executive that is aimed at enhancing the executive's performance in two areas:

1. Individual personal performance
2. Individual organizational performance

When executives are first confronted by being coached, they are not always clear about how best to use their sessions and quite unaware that it is they who set the agenda; in fact, some executives expect executive coaching to be like a one-on-one tailored training program where the executive coach initiates the agenda. Executive coaching teaches the beneficiary (coachee) to minimize, delegate, or outsource non strengths by changing ineffective behaviors or changing ineffective thinking.

The upfront purpose of executive coaching is to develop key leadership capabilities or the focus required for their current role. But it can also be used as an instrument to prepare them for the challenges of the next level. The whole coaching experience is structured to bring about effective action, performance improvement, and personal growth for the individual executive, as well as better results for the institution's core business.

An executive coach only has one item on their agenda—the client's success. This means going where it might hurt and keeping a client accountable to achieving their goals. Coaching helps people grow personally and as professionals. This growth allows them to commit completely to the success of an organization. When professional coaches work with organizations, they can turn performance management into a collaborative process that benefits both the employee and the organization.

While many executives are familiar with executive coaching, and may even have enlisted the help of external coaches at some point, few understand the right type of coaching approach required to address the challenges faced by leaders in transition situations. Many newly placed executives fail within their first two years in the position for reasons ranging from their inability to adjust to a new role and develop strong relationships to a lack of understanding of the business imperatives. What new leaders do during their first months in a new role greatly determines the extent of their success for the next several years.

What if there was a proven process to support new leaders in their role while significantly increasing return on investment and ensuring a positive economic impact for the organization?

One such process is transition coaching, an integrated and systematic process that engages and assimilates the new leader into the organization's corporate strategy and culture to accelerate productivity (Bawany 2007).

Transition coaching encompasses the goals of executive coaching but focuses on a specific niche, the newly appointed leader (someone promoted from within the ranks of the company or hired externally). Leadership transitions are among the most challenging and difficult situations executives face. Take the case of leaders who might enter a new position thinking they already have all the answers, or just the opposite, these leaders might lack a clear understanding of what to expect of the role. The goal of transition coaching is to reduce the time it takes for new leaders to make a net contribution to the organization and establish a framework for ongoing success.

Those promoted from within will have to be mindful that a smooth and effective role-to-role transition is critical to the organization's business performance. The organization depends on leaders to execute and meet objectives and has placed its bet on its internal candidates that they are better valued and have less risk. Organizations understand that successful transitions ensure future capability.

An unsuccessful transition can negatively impact an organization through poor financial results, decreased employee morale, and costly turnovers. So rather than risk this sink-or-swim gamble, organizations can improve the assimilation process through transition coaching.

If organizations use the right transition strategies when onboarding a leader, they will not only help prevent failure but will also create additional value by accelerating the new leader's effectiveness. Transition coaching engages the new leader in the organization's corporate strategy and culture to accelerate performance.

## The Potential Pitfalls of Leadership Transitions

The biggest trap that new leaders fall into is to believe that they will continue to be successful by doing what has made them successful in the past. There is an old saying, "To a person who has a hammer, everything looks like a nail." Such may also be the case with leaders who have become successful by relying on certain skills and abilities. Too often they fail to see that their new leadership role demands different skills and abilities. Thus, they fail to meet the challenges in adapting to their new role. This does not, of course, mean that new leaders should ignore their strengths. It means that they should focus first on what it will really take to be successful in the new role and discipline themselves to do things that don't come naturally if the situation demands it.

Another common trap is falling prey to the understandable anxiety the transition process evokes. Some new leaders try to take on too much, hoping that if they do enough things, something will work. Others feel they have to be seen "taking charge," and so make changes in order to put their own stamp on things. Still others experience the "action imperative"—they feel they need to be in motion, and so they don't spend enough time upfront in getting engaged in diagnosis. The result is that new leaders end up enmeshed in vicious cycles in which they make bad judgments that undermine their credibility.

New leaders are expected to "hit the ground running." They must produce results quickly while simultaneously assimilating themselves into the organization. The result is that a large number of newly recruited or promoted managers fail within the first year of starting new jobs.

From the extensive executive and transition coaching engagements over the past 20 years by the Centre of Executive Education's (CEE) panel of executive and transition coaches, we have discovered many newly promoted leaders in transition fail due to one or more of the following factors:

1. They do not fit into the organizational culture.
2. They don't build a team or become part of one.
3. They are unclear about their stakeholders', in particular their bosses', expectations.
4. They fail to execute the organization's strategic or business plans.
5. They lack the savviness in maneuvering around and managing internal politics.
6. There is no formal process to assimilate them into the organization.

A proven assimilation process is critical as it provides support to the newly hired executive and helps the organization protect its investment.

## Success Strategies for the Assimilation of New Leaders

Successful new leaders redefine their need for power and control. Team members normally value a certain amount of freedom and autonomy.

People want to influence the events around them, and they don't want to be controlled by an overbearing leader. When managers are individual contributors, they are close to the work itself, and they are the masters in control of their circumstances. Thus, their personal performance has a big effect on their satisfaction and motivation.

The situation is different when they are promoted and become leaders. Their personal contribution is less direct as they often operate behind the scenes. Leaders create frustration for everyone when they try to be involved in every project and expect team members to check in before beginning every task. World-class leaders delegate. They learn to trust. This means giving up some control. Leaders learn to live with the risks and know that someone else may do things a little differently. Every person is unique, and the person will individualize certain aspects of his or her work. When leaders don't empower and delegate, they can become ineffective and overwhelmed. In turn, team members feel underutilized and therefore less motivated.

Finally, leaders learn to transition in other critical ways. They learn how to live with occasional feelings of separation and realize that people don't always accept their decisions when faced with gut-wrenching situations. Leaders need to see the big picture. Their challenge lies in balancing the needs of many stakeholders: owners, employees, customers, and community. Because of this challenge, team members can feel alienated when unpopular decisions must be made. Leadership can be hard. It is impossible to please everyone all of the time. While the need for belonging and connecting with the group is important, leaders know the mission and vision take precedence. Sometimes a leader should make waves, champion change, and challenge people's comfort zone. Leaders may not always relish conflict, but they are not afraid of it either. Leaders are guided by standards, principles, and core values. Leaders focus on what is right, not who is right.

Leaders know they cannot make people happy. People have to take ownership and control of their own happiness. Leaders do not focus on personality factors. At times, the individual self-interests of a team member may be in opposition to the interests of the group. Leaders concentrate on shared interests and the team goal. Consequently, the driving force behind a team is a leader who treats team members with respect, while keeping the vision in mind. People are different and you have to treat people differently yet fairly.

## What Are the Skills Required for Leaders in Transition?

In the literature and research on leadership transitions and helping leaders to accelerate themselves into new roles, early findings indicate that new leaders gain leverage by putting in place the right strategies, structures, and systems. Transitions could be viewed as an engineer would approach a challenging design problem: advising leaders to identify the right goals, developing a supporting strategy, aligning the architecture of the organization, and figuring out what projects to pursue to secure early wins.

Emotional and social intelligence competencies are an essential building block in a leader's ability to establish the right climate for the business to succeed. Leaders at all levels of the organization must constantly demonstrate a high degree of emotional intelligence in their leadership role. Emotionally intelligent leaders create an environment of positive morale and higher productivity (Goleman 1998).

The critical skill sets for the next generation of leaders to be successful in their leadership roles when in transition include having cognitive readiness skills, critical thinking, multicultural communication, and effective negotiation and conflict resolution skills. The reality confronting leaders in transition is that the relationships with their bosses, peers, direct reports, and external constituencies have to be seen as good, to be a good source of leverage. These elevated relationships and the energy they can mobilize will enable the leaders to gain momentum to meet the challenges of the new roles.

This is not to say, of course, that strategies, structures, and systems are unimportant; usually, they are critical. But if the new leader hopes to put in place the right strategies, structures, and systems, they must first secure victory on the relationship front. This means building credibility with influential players, gaining agreement on goals, and securing their commitment to devote their energies to helping the new leader achieve those goals.

In the leaders' new situation, relationship management skills are critical as they aren't the only ones going through a transition. To varying degrees, many different stakeholders, both inside and outside the leader's direct line of command, are affected by the way the leader handles the new role. Inside the new leader's direct line of command are people who report directly to the leader, as well as employees from other groups. While some may feel apprehensive about the new leader's arrival, all must adjust to the leader's communication and managerial style and expectations.

Outside the new leader's direct line of command are senior executives, peers, and key external constituencies such as customers, suppliers, and distributors. The new leader will likely have no "relationship capital" with these individuals; that is, there is no existing support mechanism or obligation that the leader could draw upon. The leader will need to devote extra focus and energy in gaining their support. Leveraging through relationships is an essential foundation for effectiveness in a new leadership role.

Note that the leader's immediate boss may have strong ideas about what the leader needs to do and may have a leadership style that is markedly different from that of the leader. Put another way, leaders negotiate their way to success in their new roles.

Negotiation is a critical skill as negotiation success means proactively engaging with the leader's new boss to shape the game so that the leaders have a fighting chance of achieving the desired goals. Too many new leaders just play the game, reactively taking the situation as given and failing as a result. The alternative is to shape the game by negotiating with the leader's boss to establish realistic expectations, reach consensus on the situation, and secure enough resources. This will lay the foundation for the new leader's success.

## Transition Coaching Approach for the Development of NextGen Leaders

Transition coaching has three overall goals: (i) to accelerate the transition process by providing just-in-time advice and counsel, (ii) to prevent mistakes that may harm the business and the leader's career, and (iii) to assist the leader in developing and implementing a targeted, actionable transition plan that delivers business results (Bawany 2010).

While many of the issues covered by transition coaching are similar to those included in executive coaching, such as sorting through short- and long-term goals and managing relationships upward as well as with team members, transition coaching is focused specifically on the transition and designed to educate and challenge new leaders. The new leader and coach will have to work together to develop a transition plan, a roadmap that will define critical actions that must be taken during the first 90 days to establish credibility, secure early wins, and position the leader and team for long-term success.

The transition coaching relationship also includes regular meetings with the new leader as well as ongoing feedback. Frequently, about every four to six weeks, the coach conducts a "pulse check" of the key players, including the boss, direct reports, peers, and other stakeholders, to gather early impressions so that the new leader can make a course correction if needed.

The "Transition Readiness Assessment" for the NextGen leaders includes "cognitive readiness" competencies that include critical thinking skills, emotional and social intelligence skills, developing others with managerial coaching, cross-cultural communication, effective negotiation, and conflict management skills. The entire transition coaching process (refer to Figure 5.1) developed by the CEE provides new leaders with the guidance to take charge of their new situation, achieve alignment with the team, and ultimately move the business forward.

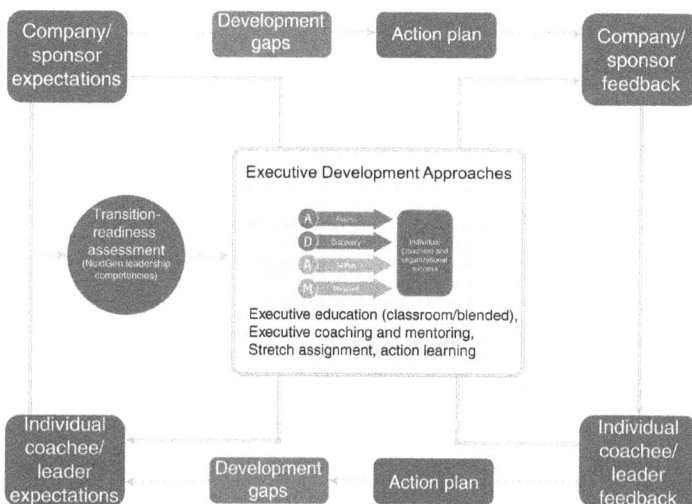

*Figure 5.1  The transition coaching framework*

## The ADAM Coaching Methodology

The ADAM coaching methodology (see Figure 5.2) developed by the CEE is a structured approach to executive coaching. This consists of a four-step process that is firmly grounded in leadership development best practices.

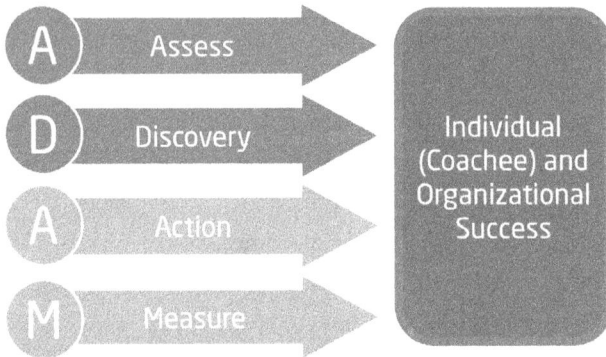

*Figure 5.2  The "ADAM" coaching methodology*

### Assess

- A series of psychometric assessments and information gathering from a series of stakeholder interviews, including the immediate manager of the new leader being coached (known as the coachee), will be conducted.
- The primary objective is to determine how the coachee's performance links to current business goals.
- An assessment of individual skills, styles, values, and leadership effectiveness forms the basis of the action plan.
- Gather background on the situation, identify the purpose of the coaching engagement, and discuss expected outcomes.
- Conduct an in-depth coachee interview, including life and career history, self-perceived behavioral and leadership strengths and shortcomings, and the desire to close the gap on weaknesses and further develop the strengths.
- Hold a tripartite session with coachee and sponsor (the coachee's immediate manager), with the objective of obtaining the senior management's commitment, and define the degree of confidentiality.
- Provide an overview of the coaching process, timetable, and parameters of the engagement.

## Discovery

- Meetings are scheduled to review the assessment data.
- The coachee will be provided with feedback on the basis of the results of the assessments that have been undertaken.
- Development objectives are discussed between the coachee and the coach to link the feedback received with the agreed business goals and professional objectives.
- On the basis of the key objectives identified, coaching activities and timelines are developed jointly between the coachee and the coach.
- The coachee, with the support of the coach, will develop an action plan that will enable the coachee to determine what to do to close the gaps in their leadership capability.
- The coach and the coachee form a working alliance where the coach provides the stimulus and environment for the coachee to prepare the action plan.
- The plan is formalized and shared by the coachee with the sponsor for agreement and support of the action plan and expected development outcomes.
- The sponsor will sign off the development plan to ensure that it aligns with the business objectives.

## Action Plan

- The coachee will implement the development plan by taking well-defined action steps and regular feedback during scheduled monthly coaching sessions with the coach. This enables the coachee to move toward measurable goals.
- "Shadowing" or observing the coachee at work (as needed and if appropriate).
- Specific actions are taken to develop the key skills and knowledge agreed to in the development plan. These actions may include:
  - Behavior modification and efforts to use new behaviors.
  - Building new skills and competencies while refining others.
  - Developing key relationships within the sponsoring organization.
  - Communication strategies for successful networking and being an ambassador for the sponsoring organization.

- The sponsor and coach communicate in person, by phone, or through e-mail, to discuss specific situations and maintain focus on the objectives of the development plan.
- There is also an opportunity for contact with the sponsor to monitor progress, as defined within the parameters of the confidentiality agreement between the sponsoring organization and the coach.

*Measure*

- A full evaluation of the coaching process and engagement based on the agreed success metrics at the beginning of the assignment yields objective measures of business results and professional outcomes for both the organization and the coachee.
- Periodically, and at the completion of the coaching program, the coachee and the coach will discuss progress against the plan and determine action plans as appropriate.
- A final tripartite coaching meeting will be held, where the results of the coaching engagement will be presented to the sponsor.
- The recommended next step for the continuous professional development of the coachee will be discussed and agreed upon with the sponsor.
- The consistent ADAM coaching delivery methodology ensures that every coachee receives the same degree of insightful business analysis, personalized consideration, and performance-driven priority.

## Case Study on Transition Coaching of the NextGen Leader

The following case study illustrates how the ADAM coaching methodology has been successfully applied in the development of the NextGen leaders.

## The Situation: Leading in a Multigenerational Workplace

A high-potential manager belonging to Gen X (born between 1964 and 1979) was promoted to the role of vice-president of operations at a major pharmaceutical organization. The manager was armed with a solid record of success in his previous role where a hands-on, controlling style with staff direct reports was an effective managerial tool. However, in his new position where he faced broad operational responsibilities, the manager needed to lead cross-functionally by bringing together departments throughout the organization, including finance, marketing, distribution, and technical operations. The makeup of employees from these various functions is those of Gen Y (born between 1980 and 1995).

With significantly more Gen Yers under his leadership, the manager's communication style was soon found to be confrontational and abrasive and often prevented him from building trusting relationships with his newly formed management team. His style also jeopardized negotiations with existing and potential key business alliances. Several of the senior management team members perceived that the manager as unwilling or unable to adapt to his new role. It was soon apparent that if left unchecked, the situation could impact the manager's career and the organization's strategic objectives. Not counting the loss of productivity, the staff replacement costs alone are expected to be substantial.

The Chief Human Resources Officer (CHRO) recommended to the CEO that an external executive coach will be a useful resource toward addressing the managerial challenges faced by this newly promoted manager. The CEO, upon reviewing the business case put up by the CHRO and the HR Business Partner, agreed to the engagement of an executive coach.

## Coaching Strategy: Assessment, Feedback, and Development of New Behavioral Skills

During the first stage of the coaching process, the manager completed a suite of psychometric assessments, including a 360-degree leadership effectiveness profile, to provide objective information about his communication and leadership style. Feedback from peers and direct reports combined with constructive communication from the CEO provided a clear insight into the manager's style, competencies, and behaviors. These data enabled the manager to see the impact his behavior had on others and how it could impact his success in building relationships and reaching business outcomes.

A developmental plan was written by the manager and reviewed with his executive coach to address gaps in areas of communication and strategic leadership. More effective techniques and approaches were role-played with the coach, and the manager was encouraged to use these new behaviors in the team and individual meetings with his boss, peers, and direct reports. He also began to use them with business associates outside the organization. The coaching goal was to increase the manager's effectiveness in all his business endeavors and to increase his ability to improve the organization's success through leading and engaging his team in a much more effective manner than before.

## Results: Tremendous Improvement in the Leader's Communication Style Observed

Key sensitive strategic alliances were successfully negotiated, resulting in a considerable new and sustained business opportunity. The manager was better able to communicate with and facilitate information transfer among his team of primarily Gen Yers. Over a duration of six months, he was able to transform them into a high-performance team. A follow-up 360-degree leadership assessment was conducted where a positive change in the manager's leadership style was perceived at all levels and by all stakeholders.

Due to the success of this coaching intervention, executive coaching is being used more broadly as a tool to enhance leadership development among the next-generation and future leaders, including the high-potential talents throughout the organization while nurturing external business alliances, resulting in the achievement of both tactical and strategic objectives of the organization.

## Reflection Questions for the Development of Next Generation of Leaders

1. What assessment processes and coaching activities/techniques are best suited for the development of the next-generation or future leaders, including the high potentials?
2. How can executive and transition coaching best relate to other forms of leadership development for next-generation leaders, such as job rotation, task force assignments, and classroom-based executive education?

3. How long should transition coaching engagement last? How frequently should executive and coach meet to achieve the desired outcomes with specific issues and within particular organizational contexts?

4. How should the organization monitor the executive, the coach, the coaching process, and coaching outcomes with the view to assess the effectiveness of the coaching engagement?

The development of the next generation of leaders includes the process of transitioning them effectively into a leadership position. This could be smoother if new leaders develop a sense of optimism and monitor and manage their outlook and perspective. Executive or transition coaching, leadership training, executive education, and the tools and systems used are very important. However, without the right outlook, new leaders, even if they are successful veterans, will experience serious difficulties and unrest.

The new leaders need to reflect on and examine their own leadership attitude and perspective and develop a plan to work on areas that need improvement. Whether a manager is moving into a new position or looking to get back on the road to success, executive or transition coaching can work to bring out the best in the new leaders through the support of a professional relationship. The relationship has to be built on a foundation of trust and confidentiality. The ability of coaches to provide leaders as an outside resource that can also act as a sounding board can help them become the successful leaders they were meant to be.

Organizations must clearly define the purpose of coaching, gauge the coaching process, and evaluate the results. Coaching is not just about providing support. Ultimately, coaching should deliver what any business needs—real results.

.

## CHAPTER 6

# Leading High-Performance NextGen Teams

## Demystifying Teams

To understand how teams deliver extra performance, it is important to distinguish between teams and other forms of working groups. That distinction turns on performance results. A working group's performance is a function of what its members do as individuals. A team's performance includes both individual results and what is called "collective work products." A collective work product is what two or more members must work on together, such as interviews, surveys, or experiments. Whatever it is, a collective work product reflects the joint, real contribution of team members.

Working groups are both prevalent and effective in large organizations where individual's accountability is most important. The best working groups come together to share information, perspectives, and insights; to make decisions that help each person do their job better; and to reinforce individual performance standards. But the focus is always on individual goals and accountabilities. Working-group members don't take responsibility for results other than their own. Nor do they try to develop incremental performance contributions requiring the combined work of two or more members (Katzenbach and Smith 1993).

Teams differ fundamentally from working groups because they require both individual and mutual accountability. Teams rely on more than group discussion, debate, and decision making; they rely more on sharing information and best-practice performance standards. Teams produce discrete work products through the joint contributions of their members. This is what makes possible performance levels greater than the sum of all the individual team members. Simply stated, a team is more than the sum of its parts.

Katzenbach and Smith (1993) stated that "a team is a small number of people with complementary skills who are committed to a common purpose, performance goals, and approach for which they hold themselves mutually accountable" (p. 45). Let's examine further this definition.

**A small number of people:** The optimal number of people in a team is generally between five and nine. While more team members bring a greater diversity of perspectives and ideas, the difficulty of consensus decision making increases dramatically. Subgroups can be created, but then the entire team is at risk of losing sight of the big picture.

**Complementary skills:** In establishing a team, it is critical to ensure that there is a mix of diverse, yet complementary, skills such as technical, functional, and interpersonal abilities.

**Committed to a common purpose:** Without a unified purpose, the team has no yardstick against which to measure its performance.

**Common performance goals:** Teams share performance goals or objectives; if a goal or objective is not achieved, the entire team is accountable. Commitment to these common performance objectives results in higher productivity and raises motivation levels.

**Common approach:** Objectives represent the "task" element of performing successfully; a common approach represents the "group process" element of working together. Neither is more important than the other, but without agreeing on how the team will interact, the chances of completing the task are pretty low!

**Mutually accountable:** This refers to the shared ownership and responsibility that is fundamental to real teamwork. If something goes wrong, there should not be any finger-pointing but rather a group effort to fix the current situation and prevent future problems. Everyone should feel free to ask for help, just as they should feel free to offer assistance. In a team, individual and team success are one and the same.

## Importance of Teams in VUCA-Driven Business Environment

Teams have become the principal building block of the strategy of successful organizations. With teams at the core of corporate strategy, the success of an organization will often depend on how well each team member operates and collaborates with others.

Today's highly disruptive, as well as volatile, uncertain, complex, and ambiguous (VUCA)–driven networked business environment not only provides a challenging environment for leaders to operate but also requires them to depend on their teams, which is critically important to getting work done (Bawany 2016b). Yet, not all teams are created equal. Some fail to perform or perform below expectations. Some start out well but later lose their focus and energy. Teams are extremely valuable if they are working well. They are very costly if they are not. It is critical for leaders to find ways to ensure their teams are working effectively and are achieving their results.

In most teams, the energies of individual members work at cross-purposes. Individuals may work extraordinarily hard, but if their efforts do not translate into a team effort, it would result in wasted energy. By contrast, when a team becomes more aligned, a commonality of direction emerges, and individual energies harmonize. You have a shared vision and an understanding of how to complement each other's efforts. As jazz musicians say, "You are in the groove" (Bawany, 2014b).

A team can have everything going for it—the brightest and most qualified people, access to resources, and a clear mission—but can still fail because it lacks group emotional intelligence.

Moreover, managers need to develop the self-awareness and interpersonal skills associated with a high level of emotional intelligence, as do teams. One way for leaders to help their teams build this capability is to understand and ensure that their teams move successfully through the stages of small-group development: membership, control, and cohesion. These stages are experienced by all teams. If teams are not well led and facilitated through them, their chances of achieving results are substantially reduced (Bawany 2014a).

## Characteristics of Effective Teams

An organization and its leaders put a great deal of effort into assembling high-performing teams. This means that the power of a team must lie in its capacity to perform at levels and deliver results greater than the sum of its parts. Considerable resources are often expended to ensure teams reach their potential. For team members, as well as other people in an organization, recognizing when a team is doing well is important. When improvement is needed, it is important to make positive changes. However, sometimes it is helpful to take a step back in order to recognize when a team is working effectively. The workings of a highly effective team are not always obvious or intuitive to everyone. Teams that are highly effective are likely to have the five characteristics described in the following.

### Well-Defined Team Charter and Operating Philosophy

The single most important ingredient in team success is a clear, common, and compelling task. The power of a team flows out of a purpose to which every team member is aligned. The task of any team is to accomplish an objective by performing at exceptional levels. Teams are not ends in themselves; rather they are a means to an end. Therefore, high-performance teams should be mission-directed and be judged by their results ultimately. This would include the team mission, purpose, values, and goals. Effective teamwork includes having a synergistic social entity that works toward a common goal or goals. Often, high-performance teams exemplify total commitment to the work and to each other.

Katzenbach and Smith (1993) stated, "Common sense suggests that teams cannot succeed without a shared purpose" (p. 2). While this may be an obvious statement, teams often form (or are developed) without a clear direction or meaning even though many researchers have explained that employees are inclined to do better when they know how to do their jobs and also why they are doing them. Teams that seek higher levels of performance should ensure that each member understands and supports the true meaning and value of their team's mission and vision. Clarifying the purpose in this manner and linking each individual's role and responsibilities is a major contributor for tapping into team potential.

### Clarity of Roles and Performance Standards of Team Members

High-performance teams are also characterized by crystal-clear roles. Every team member is clear about their particular role as well as the roles of the other team members. Roles are all about how we design, divide, and deploy work among the team. While the concept is compellingly logical, many teams find it very challenging to implement it in practice. There is often a tendency to take role definition to extremes or not take it far enough. But when they get it right, team members discover that making their combination more effective and leveraging their collective efforts is key to achieving synergistic results.

Clear performance standards are essential to high-performing teams. Such standards provide a system of accountability that also feeds into the performance ethic (Katzenbach and Smith 1993). This is an ethic that supports results for customers, employees, and shareholders, recognizing that each is of critical importance and must be balanced with great care and consideration.

Driving standards are certain pressures. These pressures include the individual's performance expectations, team pressure to perform, team leader pressure, the consequences of success or failure, and other external pressures (e.g., the larger the organization, the larger the crowd) that compel one to excel. According to Larson and LaFasto (1989), "people with high standards are those people who do ordinary things in an extraordinary way" (p. 100). When helping people reach the extraordinary, it is important to remember that setting standards must be a flexible process. Larson and LaFasto also provided three common features of developing standards of excellence: (i) setting standards that include a variety of variables; (ii) variables that include individual commitment, motivation, self-esteem, and performance; and (ii) mutual accountability and dedication to reviewing and reworking standards to keep them fresh and valuable for the team.

### Shared Norms and Culture

Like rules that govern group behavior, norms can be helpful in assisting team development and performance. For example, Jehn and Mannix (2001) proposed that high-performance teams build "open discussion" norms to promote task conflict—a type of conflict associated with high-performance teams. Other norms of high-performance teams include high levels of respect among members and a cohesive and supportive team environment. Any number of norms may exist for a given team, but high-performing teams use norms mostly to help govern behavior. In addition to having team norms, teams also benefit from organizing their team standards. As asserted by Larson and LaFasto (1989), "openly articulated or haphazardly applied, standards define those relevant and very intricate expectations that eventually determine the level of performance a team deems acceptable" (p. 95). Standards change the nature of performance by setting the bar at a new level—a level that is clearly defined.

Teams should be recognized and integrated within their organizations (Pearce and Ravlin 1987). Organizations need to clearly define their expectations and mechanisms of accountability for all teams (Sundstrom, De Meuse, and Futrell 1990). Organizational culture needs to transform shared values into behavioral norms (Blechert, Christiansen, and Kari 1987). For example, team success is fostered by a culture that incorporates shared experiences of success. In times of economic rationalizations, cultural conflicts and inconsistency may arise between the norms of maintaining the standards and adhering to the organization's mission. Team members with higher status also have less regard for team norms and may exacerbate internal conflict.

### Excellent Communication and Collaboration

Communication is the very means of cooperation or collaboration between team members. One of the primary motives for companies to implement teams is that team-based organizations are more responsive and move faster. A team, or the organization in which it resides, cannot move faster than it communicates. Fast, clear, accurate communication is a hallmark of high levels of team performance. Such teams have mastered the art of straight talk; there is little wasted motion from misunderstanding and confusion. Ideas move like quicksilver. The team understands that effective communication is key to thinking collectively and finding synergy in team solutions. As a result, team members approach communication with determined intentionality. They talk about it a lot and put a lot of effort into keeping it good and getting better.

While high-performing teams experience certain types of healthy conflict and yet are regarded as good communicators, research studies indicate that different types of communication, even different levels of perceptions of the amount of conflict, can have different types of effects. Different communication strategies appear to yield different results (including satisfaction) among those who participated, suggesting that the best forms of communication are dependent on the workgroup and their goals and objectives. Open communication in high-performing teams means a focus on coaching instead of directing (Regan 1999). The value of coaching has emerged over the past several years as a process for helping individuals think for themselves. Coaching is seen as a facilitative process where team leaders or members help facilitate the process of self- and group discovery. By utilizing coaching more frequently, individuals become less dependent and more able to take greater levels of responsibility.

### Effective Leadership

The more complex and dynamic the team's task, the more a leader is needed. Leadership should reflect the team's stage of development. Leaders need to maintain a strategic focus to support the organization's vision, facilitate goal setting, educate their team, and evaluate their teams' achievements (Proctor-Childs, Freeman, and Miller 1998). When leaders delegate responsibility appropriately, team members become more confident and autonomous and perform better.

One of the leader's roles is to ensure that the team has the right number of members with the appropriate mix and diversity of task and interpersonal and complementary skills. A balance between homogeneity and heterogeneity of members' skills, interests, and background is preferred (Hackman 1990). Homogeneous teams are composed of similar individuals who complete tasks efficiently with minimal conflict. By contrast, heterogeneous teams incorporate membership diversity and therefore facilitate innovation and problem-solving (Pearce and Ravlin 1987).

High-performing leaders usually accompany high-performance teams. High-performing teams have leaders who, when times are certain and peaceful, are able to take a proactive stance and help the team stay ahead. In fact, Regan (1999) encouraged team leaders to create a sense of distress and urgency so as not to be surprised when confronted by external crises.

Regan purported those essential leadership qualities include the following:

1. Having a vision, meaning one should see the crisis before it happens and act upon it
2. Convincing the opinion leaders of the importance of the goals at hand
3. Organizing quantitative goals
4. Being persistent in asking for the goals to be met
5. Endurance testing—leaders must remain steadfast even when their team members try to test their commitment
6. The ability to induce creativity once goals are set
7. Staying out of the team's way

Katzenbach and Smith (1993) cited six elements necessary for good team leadership:

1. Team leaders must keep the team's purpose, goals, and approach relevant and meaningful.
2. Team leaders should continue to build commitment and confidence.
3. Team leaders must ensure that their members are always enhancing their skills—including technical, problem-solving, decision-making, and interpersonal or teamwork skills.
4. Effective team leaders are skillful at managing relationships from the outside, with a focus on removing obstacles that get in the way of team performance.
5. Team leaders provide opportunities for others and are the last to seek credit.
6. Team leaders don't shy away from getting in the trenches and doing the real work.

While the authors contend that most individuals can develop effective skills to be a team leader, they suggest these components are vital for success.

## Why Do Teams Fail?

In *The Five Dysfunctions of a Team: A Leadership Fable*, Patrick Lencioni tells the story of Kathryn Petersen, DecisionTech's CEO, who faced the ultimate leadership crisis: How to unite a team that is in such disarray that it threatens to bring down the entire company. Will she succeed? Will she be fired? Lencioni's tale serves as a timeless reminder that leadership requires courage and insight (Lencioni 2002).

As difficult as it is to build a cohesive team, it is not complicated. In fact, keeping it simple is critical, whether you run the executive staff of a multinational company or head a small department in a larger organization or you are merely a member of a team that needs improvement. Lencioni reveals the five dysfunctions that are at the very heart of why teams—even the best ones—often struggle. He outlines a powerful model (see Figure 6.1) and actionable steps that can be used to overcome these common hurdles and build a cohesive, effective team (Lencioni 2002).

*Figure 6.1 Lencioni's framework of five dysfunctions of teams*

According to Lencioni, most teams unknowingly fall victim to five interrelated dysfunctions. Teams that suffer from even one of the five are susceptible to the other four. Solving all the five is required to create a high-functioning team. The five dysfunctions are displayed in a pyramid.

**Dysfunction 1: Absence of trust:** When team members do not trust one another, they are unwilling to be vulnerable within the team. It is impossible for a team to build a foundation for trust when team members are not genuinely open about their mistakes and weaknesses.

**Dysfunction 2: Fear of conflict:** Failure to build trust sets the stage for the second dysfunction. Teams without trust are unable to engage in passionate debate about ideas. Instead, they are guarded in their comments and resort to discussions that mask their true feelings.

**Dysfunction 3: Lack of commitment:** Teams that do not engage in healthy conflict will suffer from the third dysfunction. Because they do not openly express their true opinions or engage in open debate, team members will rarely commit to team decisions, though they may feign agreement in order to avoid controversy or conflict.

**Dysfunction 4: Avoidance of accountability:** A lack of commitment creates an atmosphere where team members do not hold one another accountable. Because there is no commitment to a clear action plan, team members hesitate to hold one another accountable for actions and behaviors that are contrary to the good of the team.

**Dysfunction 5: Inattention to results:** The lack of accountability makes it possible for people to put their own needs above the team's goals. Team members will focus on their own career goals or recognition for their departments to the detriment of the team.

A weakness in any one area can cause teamwork to deteriorate. The model is easy to understand and yet can be difficult to practice because it requires high levels of discipline and persistence.

## Resolving the Challenges in Leading High-Performing Teams

### Building Trust

Lencioni states that trust lies at the heart of a functioning, cohesive team and that without trust teamwork is all but impossible. As a leader, you must encourage your team members to admit their weaknesses, take risks by offering one another feedback and assistance, focus their energy on important issues, and be more willing to ask for help.

Teamwork begins by building trust. And the only way to do that is to overcome our need for invulnerability (putting up a front). Trust is the confidence among team members that their peers' intentions are good and that there is no reason to be protective or careful around the group. In essence, teammates must get comfortable being vulnerable to each other.

### Removing the Fear of Conflict

Teams that avoid conflict often do so in order to avoid hurting team members' feelings and then end up encouraging dangerous tension as a result. When team members do not openly debate and disagree with important ideas, they often turn to back-channel personal attacks, which are far nastier and more harmful than any heated argument over issues. The leader must call out sensitive issues and force the team members to work through them.

When the leader sees that people engaged in healthy conflict are uncomfortable, they should remind them that what they are doing is necessary—this can keep them encouraged. At the end of the discussion, remind the participants that the healthy conflict they just engaged in is good for the team. The leader should restate the agreements and goals arrived at and restate everyone's commitments and actions expected.

### Achieving Commitment

According to Lencioni, commitment is a function of clarity and buy-in. Leaders need to ensure that their teams make timely and clear decisions with buy-in from all team members, even those who do not agree with the decision. Teams with commitment have common objectives, move forward without hesitation, change direction when necessary, and learn from their mistakes.

To reach commitment, the five dysfunctions model recommends techniques such as establishing clear deadlines and communicating the team's goals throughout the organization. This happens through effective discussion, which is a reflection of feedback. Feedback involves active listening and understanding other team members' concerns and viewpoints. It also includes adapting communication to match the styles of other team members.

### Ensuring Accountability

Accountability requires team members to call their peers on performance or behaviors that might hurt the team. Teams where members hold one another accountable identify problems quickly by questioning one another's actions, hold one another to the same standards, and avoid needless bureaucracy around managing performance. Members of great teams improve their relationships by holding one another accountable, thus demonstrating they respect each other and have high expectations for one another's performance.

One of the best and healthiest motivators for a team is peer pressure. Clarify publicly exactly what the team needs to achieve. The enemy of accountability is ambiguity. Perform simple and regular progress reviews. Shift rewards away from individual performance to team achievement. That will create a culture of accountability because a team is unlikely to stand by quietly and fail because a peer is not pulling their weight. Once a leader has created a culture of accountability in a team, they must then be willing to become the ultimate arbiter of discipline when the team itself fails. An optimistic outlook is critical since it communicates confidence to other team members and to the rest of the organization that the team is on the right track. An optimistic team is more likely to hold one another accountable for achieving the team's goals.

### Driving Results

The ultimate dysfunction occurs when members put their own status or personal goals above the best interests of the team. Teams that focus on results minimize this type of self-centered behavior. The key is to make the collective ego greater than the individual ones. When everyone is focused on results and use them to define success, it is difficult for the ego to get out of hand. If the team loses, everyone loses. Eliminate ambiguity by having clearly agreed on and set goals. (A sports team knows at the end of the game how well it did based on the results.)

Adopt a set of common goals and measurements, then use them to make collective decisions on a daily basis. Publicly declaring the team's results and offering results-based rewards are techniques for managing this dysfunction. Without personal conscientiousness, perseverance, flexibility, and optimism, it would be difficult, if not impossible, for teams to achieve results. Innovation is another aspect of competence that is particularly important for achieving results. Teams that are creative and generate innovative products and solutions will inevitably achieve results that are superior to those of their competitors.

## The SCORE Framework for Developing High-Performance Teams

Despite society's emphasis on individuality, the critical work of business today is undertaken by teams, whether real or virtual. The success of organizations can be closely linked to how well these teams of diverse individuals perform, and it is clear that some teams do truly excel. Based on data gathered from extensive consulting engagements by the Centre for Executive Education (CEE) over a decade, several key elements have been identified as critical in high-performance organizations. These elements constitute the SCORE framework for high-performing teams (see Figure 6.2).

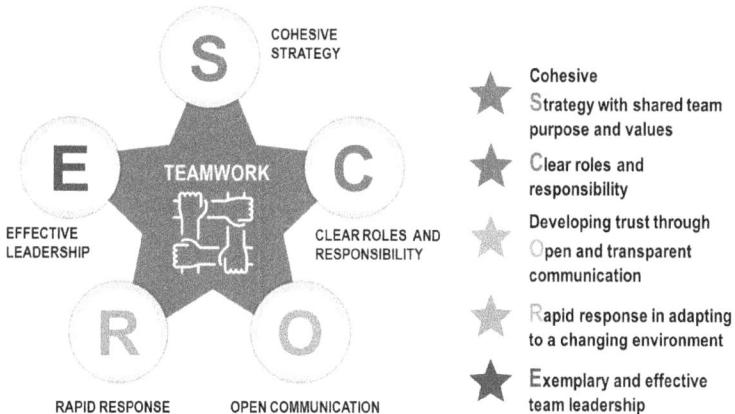

*Figure 6.2  The SCORE framework for developing high-performing teams*

A high-performing team demonstrates a high level of synergism—the simultaneous actions of separate entities that together have a greater effect than the sum of their individual efforts. For example, it is possible for a team's efforts to exemplify an equation such as $2 + 2 = 5$! High-performing teams require a complementary set of characteristics known collectively as "SCORE"—cohesive strategy, clear roles and responsibilities, open communication, rapid response, and effective leadership—as outlined in Table 6.1.

*Table 6.1 "SCORE" characteristics of high-performing teams*

| Characteristics | Descriptions |
| --- | --- |
| S: Cohesive Strategy | High-performing teams with a cohesive strategy will demonstrate why they are in existence by articulating a strong, uniting purpose that is common to all team members. They will describe how they work together by *defining team values and ground rules* (also known as team charter that will guide the team actions). Finally, they will be clear about what they do by defining key result areas (KRAs). |
| C: Establishing Clear Roles and Responsibilities | Successful teams determine overall team competencies and then clearly define individual member's roles and responsibilities. High-performing teams examine each individual's responsibilities in terms of the key competencies of the role, resulting in an accurate understanding of each member's accountability and contribution to the team. |
| O: Developing Open Communication and Trust | Communication is the key component in facilitating successful team performance; its lack limits team success. Effective communication includes *flexing and adapting one's style of communication* to suit the other team members. In addition, a cohesive culture is attained when interpersonal interactions flow smoothly and individual differences are also respected and leveraged to enhance overall team functioning. |
| R: Rapid Response to Problem-Solving and Decision Making | A high-performing team responds quickly, as necessary, to changes in the environment, by shifting its members' mental models with creativity and "outside-the-box" thinking. When faced with a problem, these teams brainstorm possible solutions and create innovative resolutions leveraging on NextGen leadership competencies, including *cognitive readiness and critical thinking skills*. |
| E: Exemplary and Effective Leadership | An effective team leader is able to adjust their leadership style (leveraging on *Results-Based Leadership and Situational Leadership Frameworks*) as necessary depending on the task at hand and the skill level of each team member performing that task. The team leader also demonstrates effective emotional and social intelligence skills as well as plays a critical role in raising team morale by *providing positive feedback and coaching team members* (managerial coaching skills) to improve performance. Finally, the team leader takes an active role in guiding the team through each stage of team development by using team-building activities and celebrating successes. |

In high-performing teams, leadership shifts during the stages of team development on the basis of team needs. Unlike organizational leadership, which remains somewhat constant, team leadership can shift from very directing, when the team is being formed, to more delegating, when the team is functioning effectively. When you have assessed your team's current performance level and needs, you will be ready to move on to building your dream team in whatever SCORE category you choose to begin.

# Case Study: Turnaround of a Highly Dysfunctional Team

A leading Fortune 500 information technology (IT) company dispatched a team of highly qualified and experienced IT engineers to deliver a large-scale strategic project for one of their clients in the mobile telecommunications industry. Sustaining market leadership for this client was critical to the success of this organization. However, high employee turnover, especially among the mission-critical talents, had created misalignment in what was once a strong performing team. Moreover, as competitors encroached, relationship management was critical with this strategic account. All this transcended the sound technical expertise of the IT engineers who demonstrated that a primary form of communication was e-mail. There was a lack of direction and clarity on the respective project team members' role and responsibilities compounded by the relatively ineffective team communication, which resulted in frequent conflict leading to poor performance and results.

The SCORE framework was introduced through the facilitation of a series of team effectiveness meetings and workshops; the project team achieved breakthrough results in customer satisfaction and enhanced company, employee, and operational values. The team's key performance indicators (KPIs) were achieved with shortened response times and improved communication project delivery within the allocated budget.

The team's emotional intelligence was enhanced and relationship management became second nature as team members became more expansive, leading to the early exploration of new business opportunities. A post–customer satisfaction survey confirmed the acknowledgment of the value that the client provided to its customer.

Finally, the organization preserved its strategic account and strengthened the customer relationship, thereby sustaining market leadership. The project team's ultimate proof of transformation was its unanimous decision to distribute among all team members annual performance bonuses previously assigned to a select few. This presents some evidence that high-performance teams impact not only the organization and marketplace but above all the gratified individuals that constitute them.

## Best-Practice Toolkit: The Five-Step "AGREE" Framework to Achieve Collaboration

The CEE has developed the five-step AGREE process (see Figure 6.3) for achieving commitment to collaboration at the workplace as well as resolving conflict and negotiation situations driven by the use of communication skills.

**1 ACKNOWLEDGE:**
set the tone for a productive interaction

**GROUND RULES:**
clearer expectations and greater comfort  **2**

**3 REALITY:**
understand the context of the issues on hand

**EXPLORE:**
brainstorming and exploring multiple options  **4**

**5 EXECUTE:**
implement or execute the best solution effectively

*Figure 6.3 The "AGREE" framework to achieve team collaboration*

### A: Acknowledge

The critical first step in achieving collaboration or resolving conflict is for all parties to acknowledge that a conflict exists. This is particularly important when any of the involved parties prefer a management style that is characteristic of conflict avoidance. Acknowledging that a difference in the way of working or conflict exists and inviting parties to collaborate help set the tone for a productive interaction.

Example: "I sense that we see this issue very differently, and I believe it is an important matter. Would it be helpful, from your perspective, to spend some time focusing on this? Who else should we involve to help us find a workable solution or work toward resolving this?"

## G: Ground Rules

Ground rules help establish the tone, climate, and time frame for a discussion toward a collaboration process. By establishing rules upfront, the parties begin negotiations with clearer expectations and a greater degree of comfort.

Examples: Listen to understand. Question to clarify. Maximize participation. Silence means assent. Speak for yourself. Be respectful.

## R: Reality

Establishing the context and understanding the current reality related to the issues or conflict in question is the most critical step in achieving collaboration. It is used to move from the destructive side of collaboration (blame or winning at the other person's expense) to the constructive side (resolving problems). In this phase, each person or stakeholder clearly articulates their understanding of the other person's position and must consciously put any emotion aside and reconsider the situation from all perspectives.

Example: "If I am understanding you correctly, you are saying. . . ."

## E: Explore

People rarely see a need for numerous options because each party already knows the right option, which is their own position. Brainstorming and exploring multiple options gives parties room to negotiate and support a problem-solving focus. The goal is to create as many options as possible that are responsive to the interests of all parties.

Example: "What do you think are the possible alternatives to resolve this challenge or issue?"

## E: Execute

Sometimes the best option is readily apparent and satisfactory to all parties and the decision is made. More often, the parties select those options with the most potential and continue to explore them. Use of relevant objective criteria provides an independent basis for decision making by avoiding the will or power of either party. Once the best solution has been identified and agreed upon, the final step will be to implement or execute it effectively. Have a follow-up discussion regularly to enhance the collaboration.

Example: Possible objective criteria include cost, timeline, and customer demand.

# Conclusion

The success of a team should be measured at regular intervals so that team spirit can be encouraged, either through celebrating achievements or through sharing problems. In terms of measuring success, it is perhaps easier to gauge the progress of a sports team than it is to rate the performance of work-based teams; for example, the performance of a sports team can usually be tracked by league tables.

Working as part of a successful team makes work enjoyable. It provides employees with a supportive work environment and enables them to address in a constructive way any conflict that might arise. In high-performing teams, leadership shifts during the stages of team development on the basis of team needs. Unlike organizational leadership, which remains somewhat constant, team leadership can shift from very directing, when the team is being formed, to more delegating, when the team is functioning effectively. To transform into high-performance teams, easily implementable frameworks such as SCORE and AGREE can help with achieving that end goal.

# CHAPTER 7

# Leadership 4.0—The Future of NextGen Leadership

In recent times, the world has moved well beyond basic and enhanced process automation. It is entering an era of cognitive automation leveraging on artificial intelligence and robotics that the World Economic Forum termed as the "Fourth Industrial Revolution" (also known as Industry 4.0) (Bawany 2019).

To ensure their readiness toward digital business transformation, most organizations would deploy state-of-the-art technology. But do they have a relevant structure and the right talent in place? Will they be equipped to attract, develop, and retain digital talent? Do they know what it takes to lead in a digital era, which is expected to get only more intense in the coming years? These are questions that many, if not all, organizations are grappling with as they seek to succeed in developing their NextGen leaders in the digital era.

Organization and leadership transformation is expected to continue in the near future in view of the insurmountable challenges posed by a highly disruptive, digital, and volatile, uncertain, complex, and ambiguous (VUCA)–driven Industry 4.0.

No change happens without challenges, and most successful organizations will have transformational leaders at the helm to navigate those obstacles—the test is finding and developing these next-generation or future leaders today. Organizations that understand this need to place a high priority on leadership development. In turn, they can expect greater revenue return, stronger market position, and better growth potential than organizations that don't leverage leadership development as an avenue for success.

In view of these challenges in the future, there are several issues that need to be addressed in the development of NextGen leaders. First, the organizations need to continuously reinvent themselves. In light of the future challenges, they would need to reassess their organizational purpose, strategy, structure, and leadership development approaches. Second, organizations need to reassess their individual future leader's capability to drive transformation. This includes the development and implementation of intrapreneurial initiatives or innovation projects and the organizational capability to support such transformations.

At the Centre for Executive Education (CEE), as part of the ongoing dialogue with CEOs and C-Suite business leaders, it has been found that those who invest in the development of NextGen leaders ensure that their future leaders can drive the transformation of the companies and businesses that they lead. As well-functioning organizations typically recruit their senior leaders from within, the development of leadership capability is a way to organize transformation over the long run.

It is evident that conventional leadership development practices are no longer adequate. Organizations globally need to incorporate the Next-Gen leadership competencies in order to address the development needs of their future leaders. This expanded group of upcoming leaders need to have a broader skill set, one that equips them to think and act globally in the digital and VUCA-driven business environment. They must do so while embracing cross-cultural diversity and cultivating collaborative relationships within and outside their walls. These are the hallmarks of the mindset needed to develop effective NextGen leaders.

At the same time, globalization leads to the emergence of more complex organizations. There is a trend to move away from the classical hierarchical model to one that allows flexibility and rapid response to the evolving challenges in the marketplace where crucial relations and decisions need not necessarily involve the headquarters. Hence, both internal and external changes are required that would enhance the ability of an organization to adapt. The ability to drive such changes is related to innovativeness and entrepreneurship.

## Redefining Leadership 4.0

Leadership 4.0 is about leaders creating their own digital transformation strategy and ensuring that it is aligned with the business and growth plans of their organizations. It is critical that there must be commitment to and sense of ownership on the part of the various stakeholders, including the boards of directors and senior leadership. For those willing to embrace this new world, it presents huge opportunities to be leveraged, offering the prospect of new markets and new customers. However, to accomplish this, it would be crucial for the next generation of leaders to develop the relevant knowledge and skills, which in turn will help them evolve into a digitally transformed leader (Bawany 2019).

Leadership 4.0 is also about a "digital leader" who can build teams, keep people connected and engaged, and drive a culture of innovation, risk tolerance, and continuous improvement. Even as digital disruption is now sweeping across every major industry, regrettably leadership capabilities are not keeping pace.

As part of the cognitive transformation, digital leaders' thinking differently and applying innovative thinking is one step in creating an innovative, organizational response to changes resulting from Industry 4.0. What is required is to develop a culture of innovation throughout the organization where innovative and creative thinking is applied to solve problems and develop new products and services.

Studies have shown that the climate for creativity in organizations is directly attributable to leadership behavior. What this means is that leaders must act in ways that promote and support organizational innovation. They must demonstrate specific competencies, skills, and behaviors, known as cognitive readiness, which would support an innovative and knowledge-driven learning organization.

This new normal is challenging leaders to find new ways to lead their organizations and achieve sustained success as reflected in the 2019 *Trends in Executive Development: A Benchmark Report,* published by the Executive Development Associates (EDA), a pioneer in executive development. (Hagemann et al. 2019)

The impact of digital disruption has to be managed alongside the more general VUCA operating conditions of recent years. An ability to calculate and manage/mitigate risk will, therefore, be another key requirement of leaders seeking to propel their organizations into the digital age. Navigating a course through these difficult conditions may also force leaders to look at their individual leadership style and decide whether it needs to be adjusted.

According to the latest EDA research, in response to the question, "As you look down in the organization at the next generation of leadership talent (the ones who are most likely to fill executive level positions in the 3–5 years), what capabilities, skills, knowledge, attitudes, and competencies are most lacking?", survey respondents indicated that the top 5 competencies most lacking in the next generation of leaders are as follows (Hagemann et al. 2019):

1. Ability to attract, develop, and retain high-quality talent needed to achieve the business objectives
2. Ability to create a compelling vision and engage others around it
3. Ability to inspire others
4. Ability to deliver results or is results oriented
5. Ability to manage the stress and demands of a real-time overloaded leadership environment

## Embrace and Encourage Innovation

Corporations need to offer some flexibility in order to adapt to digital platforms and strategies. Great talent thrives on impact and innovation—the same things a company needs to survive in the future. If a company prioritizes its processes over smart and impactful contributions, it is setting itself up to lose creative up-and-comers, not to mention potentially falling behind the competition. Innovators and change-makers set bold ambitions and work on the edge of possibility. Employees working in the trenches often find the most efficient solutions, and it is often best to follow their lead.

A good leader needs to be open to creative employee solutions and innovations, rather than trying to put limits on innovation. For example, at Google, one of its most famous management philosophies is something called "20% time." Employees are encouraged to spend 20 percent of their time working on what they think will most benefit Google, in addition to their regular projects. This empowers them to be more creative and innovative. In some ways, the idea of 20 percent time is more important than the reality of it as it operates somewhat outside the lines of formal management oversight, and always will because the most talented and creative people cannot be forced to work.

Corporations need to set the stage for innovation by breaking down barriers and empowering the workforce. They need to give employees the opportunity to venture out of their standard career paths and customize their jobs to align with their personal and evolving skill sets, interests, and career goals. They need to provide a more open work environment with increased information transparency and trust in expertise by changing the default content and process working mechanisms from private to public.

# Conclusion

Leadership 4.0 is, in fact, more important in times of change than at any other, but its nature has perhaps changed somewhat to take into account the more collaborative nature of the digital workplace. The digital revolution not only opens up new opportunities for how organizations arrange work and structure themselves but also leads to new ways of working and leading high-performing teams.

Although some traditional leadership capabilities still remain critical to successfully lead in the digital era (e.g., creating and communicating a clear vision, motivating and empowering others), there are also new requirements for leaders at all levels of the organization. These demand a dynamic combination of a new mindset and behaviors as well as digital knowledge and skills that are critical to leading teams in the digital era.

As digital technology impacts the entire organization, it requires effective leadership at all levels to drive the digital strategy going forward. As digital transformation expands across the organization and the "war for talent" continues, organizations need to consider a more structured approach to building a healthy leadership pipeline with the necessary capabilities to lead in the digital era. They can do this by placing potential leaders in positions that stretch them beyond their current competencies and skills and by coaching them and supporting them on building new digital capabilities as rapidly as possible.

Maybe one day in the future everyone in every organization will be a leader, but for now, the traditional practice of leadership remains as vital as it ever was.

# References

American Management Association. 2007. *The High-Performance Organization Survey on How to Build a High-performance Organization: A Global Study of Current Trends and Future Possibilities 2007–2017.* New York, NY: AMA.

Bawany, S. 2019. "Leadership 4.0: How ready are you to be a Digital Leader?" *Leadership Excellence Essentials* 36, no. 2, pp. 28–30.

Bawany, S. 2018a. *Developing a High-Performance Organization in a VUCA World.* New York, NY: Expert Insights Series by Business Express Press (BEP) Inc. LLC.

Bawany, S. 2018b. *Identifying, Assessing and Selecting NextGen Leaders.* New York, NY: Expert Insights Series by Business Express Press (BEP) Inc. LLC.

Bawany, S. 2018c. *Leading in a Disruptive VUCA World.* New York, NY: Expert Insights Series by Business Express Press (BEP) Inc. LLC.

Bawany, S. 2018d. *Leading the Digital Transformation of Organizations.* New York, NY: Expert Insights Series by Business Express Press (BEP) Inc. LLC.

Bawany, S. 2018e. *What Makes a Great Nextgen Leader?* New York, NY: Expert Insights Series by Business Express Press (BEP) Inc. LLC.

Bawany, S. 2018f. *Development and Coaching of NextGen Leaders,* New York, NY: Expert Insights Series by Business Express Press (BEP) Inc. LLC.

Bawany, S. 2017. "The Art and Practice of Servant Leadership: Importance of Empathy as an Emotional & Social Intelligence Competency for Servant Leaders." *Leadership Excellence Essentials* 34, no. 11, pp. 34–35.

Bawany, S. 2016a. "Leading in a VUCA Business Environment: Leveraging on Cognitive Readiness and RBL for Organizational Success." *Leadership Excellence Essentials* 33, no. 7, pp. 39–40.

Bawany, S. 2016b. "NextGen Leaders for a VUCA World." *Leadership Excellence Essentials* 33, no. 7, pp. 39–40.

Bawany, S. 2015a. "Results-based Leadership: Putting Your Employees First before Customer & Profits." *Leadership Excellence Essentials* 32, no. 5, pp. 22–23.

Bawany, S. 2015b. "What Makes a Great Leader? The Emotional & Social Intelligence Competencies of Highly Effective Leaders." *Leadership Excellence Essentials* 32, no. 12, pp. 5–6.

Bawany, S. 2014a. "Building High Performance Organizations with Results-based Leadership (RBL) Framework." *Leadership Excellence Essentials* 31, no. 11, pp. 46–47.

Bawany, S. 2014b. "Building High Performance Teams Using SCORE Framework." *Talent Management Excellence* 2, no. 4, pp. 23–24.

Bawany, S. 2014c. "Managing Talent: Demystifying Board's Role in Talent Management." *Talent Management Excellence Essentials* 2, no. 9, pp. 18–19.

Bawany, S. 2014d. "Transforming the NextGen Leaders: Leadership Pipeline for Succession Planning." *Leadership Excellence Essentials* 31, no. 7, pp. 30–31.

Bawany, S. September, 2010. "Maximizing the Potential of Future Leaders: Resolving Leadership Succession Crisis with Transition Coaching." In *Coaching in Asia—The First Decade*, eds. D. Wright, A, Leong, K.E. Webb and S. Chia. Singapore: Candid Creation Publishing LLP.

Bawany, S. 2007. "Winning the War for Talent." In *Human Capital*, 54–57. September – October 2017 Issue. Singapore: Singapore Human Resources Institute.

Bawany, S., and A. Bawany. 2015. "Inspiring Your Future Workforce: How to lead and engage Gen Y and Z effectively." *Talent Management Excellence Essentials* 32, no. 1, pp. 14–16.

Bennis, W. 1989. *On Becoming a Leader*. New York, NY: Addison Wesley.

Blechert T. F., M.F. Christiansen, and N. Kari. 1987. "Intraprofessional Team Building." *American Journal of Occupational Therapy* 41, no. 9, pp. 576–82.

Bolt, J.F., and B. Hagemann. July 9, 2009. "Lessons from the Front Line – Harvesting Tomorrow's Leaders." *Training and Development*, pp. 53–57 July 2009 Issue.

Boyatzis, R.E. 1982. *The Competent Manager: A Model for Effective Performance*. New York, NY: Wiley.

Boyatzis, R.E. 1994. "Rendering Unto Competence the Things that are Competent." *American Psychologist* 49, no. 1, pp. 64–66.

Boyatzis, R.E. 2006. "Core Competencies in Coaching Others to Overcome Dysfunctional Behavior." In *Linking Emotional Intelligence and Performance at Work: Current Research Evidence with Individuals and Groups,* ed. R.E. Boyatzis. Mahwah, NJ: Lawrence Erlbaum Associates Publishers.

Boyatsiz, R.E. 2008. "Competencies in the 21st Century." *Journal of Management Development* 27, no. 1, pp. 5–12.

Burdett, J.O. 1998. "Forty 'Things Every Manager Should Know About Coaching.'" *Journal of Management and Development* 17, no. 2, pp. 142–52.

Campbell, M., and R. Smith. 2010. *High Potential Talent: A View from Inside the Leadership Pipeline.* Colorado Springs, CO: Center for Creative Leadership.

Cappelli, P. 2008. *Talent on Demand: Managing Talent in an Age of Uncertainty.* Boston, MA: Harvard Business Press.

Chamorro-Premuzic, T., S. Adler, and R.B. Kaiser. October 3, 2017. "What Science Says About Identifying High-Potential Employees." *Harvard Business Review.*

Charan, R. 2017. *The High-Potential Leader: How to Grow Fast, Take on New Responsibilities, and Make an Impact,* 1st ed. Hoboken, NJ: Wiley Publishers.

Charan, R., S. Drotter, and J. Noel. 2001. *The Leadership Pipeline: How to Build a Leadership Powered Company.* San Francisco, CA: Jossey-Bass.

Christensen, C.M. 1997. *The Innovator's Dilemma: When New Technologies Cause Great Firms to Fail.* Boston, MA: Harvard Business School Press.

Christensen, C.M., M. Raynor, and R. McDonald. 2015. "What Is Disruptive Innovation?" *Harvard Business Review* 93, no. 12, pp. 44–53.

Collins, J.C., and J. I. Porras. (1994). *Built to Last: Successful Habits of Visionary Companies.* New York, NY: Harper Business.

Conger, J.A., and R.M. Fulmer. 2003. "Developing your Leadership Pipeline." *Harvard Business Review* 8, no. 12, pp. 76–85.

Corporate Leadership Council. 2005. *Realizing the full potential of rising talent (Volume 1): A Quantitative Analysis of the Identification and Development of High Potential Employees.* Washington, D. C.: Corporate Executive Board.

Corporate Leadership Council. 2010. *Six Mistakes that Drive Away your Rising Stars.* Washington, D.C.: Corporate Executive Board.

de Waal, A.A. 2007. "The Characteristics of a High-Performance Organization." *Business Strategy Series* 8, no. 3, pp. 179–85.

Doheny, M., V. Nagali, and F. Weig. May, 2012. "Agile Operations for Volatile Times." *McKinsey Quarterly.*

Dries, N., and R. Pepermans. 2008. "'Real' High Potential Careers: An Empirical Study into the Perspectives of Organizations and High Potentials." *Personnel Review* 37, no. 1, pp. 85–108.

Edwards, L. 2003. "Coaching the Latest Buzzword or a Truly Effective Management Tool?" *Industrial and Commercial Training* 35, no. 7, pp. 298–300.

Erickson, T. February, 2010. "Are 'High Potential' Programs an Anachronism?" *Harvard Business Review.* Retrieved December 18, 2018. http://blogs.hbr.org/erickson/2010/02/is_high_potential_an_anachroni.html

Evered, R.D., and J.C. Selman. 1989. "Coaching and the Art of Management." *Organizational Dynamics* 18, no. 2, pp. 16–33.

Fayol, H. 1949. *General and Industrial Management.* London, UK: Pitman.

Fernández-Aráoz, C., B. Groysberg, and N. Nohria. 2011. "How to Hang on to your High Potentials." *Harvard Business Review* 89, pp. 76–83.

Gallup. 2018. *The Engaged Workplace: A Highly Engaged Workforce Means the Difference Between a Company that Outperforms its Competitors and One that Fails to Grow.* https://www.gallup.com/services/190118/engaged-workplace.aspx, (accessed November 16, 2018).

Goleman, D. 1988. *What Makes a Leader?* Harvard Business Review, November—December, pp. 93–102

Goleman, D. 1995. *Emotional Intelligence.* New York, NY: Bantam Books.

Goleman, D. 1998. *Working with Emotional Intelligence.* New York, NY: Bantam Books.

Goleman, D. March–April, 2000. "Leadership that Gets Results." *Harvard Business Review*, pp 15–29.

Goleman, D. 2006. *Social Intelligence: The New Science of Human Relationships*. New York, NY: Bantam Books.

Hackman, J.R., ed. 1990. *Groups that Work (and Those That Don't)*. San Francisco, CA: Jossey-Bass.

Hagemann, B., and S. Bawany. 2016. "Enhancing Leadership and Executive Development - Latest Trends & Best Practices." *Leadership Excellence Essentials* 33, no. 3, pp. 9–11.

Hagemann, B., S. Bawany, H. Ishikawa, L. Korver and S. Terrel, 2016. *Research on Trends in Executive Development: A Benchmark Report*. Oklahoma City, OK: Executive Development Associates (EDA); Pearson TalentLens and Performance Assessment Network (PAN).

Hagemann, B., and S. Bawany, J. Parisi, T. Clayton and S. Dannemiller, 2019. *Trends in Executive Development: 2019 Benchmark Report*. Oklahoma City, OK: Executive Development Associates, Inc. (EDA) & BTS, USA.

Hagemann, B., S. Vetter, and J. Maketa. 2017. *Leading with Vision: the Leader's Blueprint for Creating a Compelling Vision and Engaging the Workforce*. Boston, MA: Nicholas Brealey Publishing.

Hogan, J., R. Hogan, and R.B. Kaiser. 2011. "Managerial Derailment." In *APA Handbook of Industrial and Organizational Psychology*, ed. S. Zedeck, Vol. 3, 555–75. Washington, D.C.: American Psychological Association.

Hollenbeck, G.P., and M.W. McCall. 2001. "What Makes a Successful Global Executive?" *Business Strategy Review* 12, pp. 49–56.

Jhen, K.A., and E.A. Mannix. 2001. "The Dynamic -Nature of Conflict: A Longitudinal Study of Intragroup Conflict and Group Performance." *Academy of Management Journal* 44, no. 2, pp. 238–51.

Johansen, R. 2011. *Leaders Make the Future: Ten New Leadership Skills for an Uncertain World*, 2nd ed. San Francisco, CA: Berrett-Koehler Publishers.

Katzenbach, J.R., and D.K. Smith. 1993. *The Wisdom of Teams: Creating the High-performance Organization*. New York, NY: Harper Business.

King, P., and J. Eaton. 1999. "Coaching for Results." *Industrial and Commercial Training* 31, no. 4, pp. 145–48.

Kirby, J. July–August, 2005. "Toward a Theory of High Performance." *Harvard Business Review* 83, pp. 30–39.

Konczak, L., and Foster, J. October, 2009. *Developing Next-generation Leaders: High Priority on High Potentials*. Society of Industrial and Organisational Psychologists—TIP. http://www.siop.org/tip/oct09/04konczak.aspx (accessed March 2, 2019).

Larson, C.E., and F. M. J. LaFasto. 1989. *Teamwork: What Must Go Right, What Can Go Wrong*. Newbury Park, CA: Sage Publications.

Lencioni, P.M. 2002. *The Five Dysfunctions of a Team, A Leadership Fable*. San Francisco, CA: Jossey-Bass.

Levenson, A. 2011. *Measuring the Impact of a Managerial Competency System: Does Identifying and Rewarding Potential Leaders Improve Organizational Performance?* Cambridge, MA: Center for Effective Organizations.

Liu, J., A. Srivastava, and H.S. Woo. 1998. "Transference of Skills between Sports and Business." *Journal of European Industrial Training* 22, no. 3, pp. 93–112.

Manchester Inc. January 4, 2001. "Executive Coaching Yields Return on Investment of Almost Six Times Its Costs." *Business Wire*, pp. 2–3.

Martin, J., and Schmidt, C. May, 2010. "How to Keep Your Top Talent." *Harvard Business Review*, pp. 54–61.

McCall, M.W. 2010. "Recasting Leadership Development." *Industrial and Organizational Psychology* 3, pp. 3–19.

McCall, M., M. Lombardo, and A. Morrison. 1988. *The Lessons of Experience*. Lexington, MA: Lexington Books.

McClelland, D.C. 1973. "Testing for Competence Rather than for 'Intelligence.'" *American Psychologist* 28, pp. 1–14.

McClelland, D.C. 1994. "The Knowledge-testing-educational Complex Strikes Back." *American Psychologist* 49, pp. 66–69.

McClelland, D.C. 1998. "Identifying Competencies with Behavioral-event Interviews." *Psychological Science* 9, pp. 331–39.

McClelland, D.C., and R.E. Boyatzis. 1982. "Leadership Motive Pattern and Long-term Success in Management." *Journal of Applied Psychology* 67, pp. 737–43.

McCracken, H. 2017. Satya Nadella Rewrites Microsoft's Code, Fast Company, Long Read, 18 September 2017. https://www.fastcompany.com/40457458/satya-nadella-rewrites-microsofts-code, (accessed October 10, 2018).

Michaels, E., H. Handfield-Jones, and B. Axelrod. 2001. *The War for Talent*. Boston, MA: Harvard Business School, McKinsey & Co.

O'Shaughnessy, S. 2001. "Executive Coaching the Route to Business Stardom." *Industrial and Commercial Training* 33, no. 6, pp. 194–97.

Parker-Wilkins, V. 2006. "Business Impact of Executive Coaching: Demonstrating Monetary Value." *Industrial and Commercial Training* 38, no. 3, pp. 122–27.

Parsloe, E., and M. Wray. 2000. *Coaching & Mentorship: Practical Methods to Improve Learning*. London, UK: Kogan.

Pearce J.A., and E.C. Ravlin. 1987. "The Design and -Activation of Self-Regulating Work Groups." *Human Relations* 40, no. 11, pp. 751–82.

Peters, T., and R. Waterman. 1982. *In Search Of Excellence*. New York, NY: Warner Books.

Proctor-Childs T., M. Freeman, and C. Miller. 1998. "Visions of Teamwork: The Realities of an Interdisciplinary Approach." *British Journal of -Therapy and Rehabilitation* 5, no. 12, pp. 616–35.

Ready, D.A., J.A. Conger, and L.A. Hill. June, 2010. "Are You a High Potential?" *Harvard Business Review* 88, pp. 78–84.

Regan, M.D. 1999. *The Journey to Teams: A Practical Step-by-Step Implementation Plan*. New York, NY: Holden Press.

Salovey, P., and J.D. Mayer. 1990. "Emotional Intelligence." *Imagination, Cognition, and Personality* 9, pp. 185–211.

Schippmann, J. 2010. "Employee Engagement: A Focus on Leaders." In *Strategy-driven Talent Management*, eds. R. Silzer and B.E. Dowell, 439–59. San Francisco, CA: Jossey-Bass.

Schwab, K. 2017. *The Fourth Industrial Revolution*. New York, NY: Crown Publishing Group.

Scott, J.C., and D.H. Reynolds, eds. 2010. *The Handbook of Workplace Assessment: Evidenced-based Practices for Selecting and Developing Organizational Talent*. San Francisco, CA: Jossey–Bass.

Silzer, R., and A.H. Church. 2009a. "The Pearls and Perils of Identifying Potential." *Industrial and Organisational Psychology* 2, pp. 377–412.

Silzer, R., and A.H. Church. 2009b. "The Potential of Potential." *Industrial and Organizational Psychology* 2, pp. 446–52.

Silzer, R, and A. Church. 2010. "Identifying and Assessing High-potential Talent: Current Organizational Practices." In *Strategy-Driven Talent*

*Management: A Leadership Imperative*, eds. R.F. Silzer and B.E. Dowell, 213–79. San Francisco, CA: Jossey-Bass.

Silzer, R.F., and B.E. Dowell. 2010. "Strategic Talent Management." In *Strategy-Driven Talent Management: A Leadership Imperative*, eds. R.F. Silzer and B.E. Dowell, 3–72. San Francisco, CA: Jossey-Bass.

Stoddard, N., and C. Wyckoff. April 9, 2009. "Pick a CEO who Truly Fits the Company." *Forbes*.

Sundstrom, E., K.P. De Meuse, and D. Futrell. 1990. "Work Teams: Applications and Effectiveness." *American Psychologist* 45, no. 2, pp. 120–33.

Watkins, M. 2003. *The First 90 Days*. Boston, MA: Harvard Business School Press.

Whiteman, W.E. 1998. *Training and Educating Army Officers for the 21st Century: Implications for the United States Military Academy*. Fort Belvoir, VA: Defense Technical Information Center.

Wilson, C. 2004. "Coaching and Coach Training in the Workplace." *Industrial and Commercial Training* 36, no. 3, pp. 96–98.

# About the Author

***Sattar Bawany*** is the chief executive officer and certified C-Suite Master Executive Coach of the Centre for Executive Education (CEE). He has over 30 years' international business management experience, including 20 years in executive coaching, group facilitation, and leadership development and training with global management consulting firms. In addition to his business and consulting career, he has over 15 years of concurrent academic experience as an adjunct professor teaching senior executives international business strategies and human resource courses at various leading universities.

Sattar is an astute advisor to executives who need to know how they are perceived and want to focus on what is most important in their professional and personal lives. He has coached a range of leaders, from CEOs to senior vice presidents, and high-potential managers.

Sattar holds an executive MBA from Golden Gate University and a bachelor in business administration (marketing) from Curtin University.

# Index

## OTHER TITLES IN THE HUMAN RESOURCE MANAGEMENT AND ORGANIZATIONAL BEHAVIOR COLLECTION

- *How Successful Engineers Become Great Business Leaders* by Paul Rulkens
- *Creating a Successful Consulting Practice* by Gary W. Randazzo
- *Skilling India: Challenges and Opportunities* by S. Nayana Tara and Sanath Kumar
- *Redefining Competency Based Education: Competence for Life* by Nina Morel and Bruce Griffiths
- *No Dumbing Down: A No-Nonsense Guide for CEOs on Organization Growth* by Karen D. Walker
- *From Behind the Desk to the Front of the Stage: How to Enhance Your Presentation Skills* by David Worsfold
- *The New World of Human Resources and Employment: How Artificial Intelligence and Process Redesign is Driving Dramatic Change* by Tony Miller
- *Our Glassrooms: Perceptiveness and Its Implications for Transformational Leadership* by Dhruva Trivedy
- *Virtual Vic: A Management Fable* by Laurence M. Rose
- *What Millennials Really Want From Work and Life* by Yuri Kruman
- *Temperatism, Volume II: Doing Good Through Business With a Social Conscience* by Carrie Foster
- *Practicing Management* by Alan S. Gutterman
- *Practicing Leadership* by Alan S. Gutterman
- *Women Leaders: The Power of Working Abroad* by Sapna Welsh and Caroline Kersten
- *Breakthrough: Career Strategies for Women's Success* by Saundra Stroope
- *Comparative Management Studies* by Alan S. Gutterman
- *Cross-Cultural Leadership Studies* by Alan S.Gutterman
- *No Cape Required: Empowering Abundant Leadership* by Bob Hughes and Helen Caton Hughes
- *Leading Organizational Transformation* by Linda Mattingly

## Announcing the Business Expert Press Digital Library

*Concise e-books business students need for classroom and research*

This book can also be purchased in an e-book collection by your library as

- *a one-time purchase,*
- *that is owned forever,*
- *allows for simultaneous readers,*
- *has no restrictions on printing, and*
- *can be downloaded as PDFs from within the library community.*

Our digital library collections are a great solution to beat the rising cost of textbooks. E-books can be loaded into their course management systems or onto students' e-book readers.
The **Business Expert Press** digital libraries are very affordable, with no obligation to buy in future years. For more information, please visit **www.businessexpertpress.com/librarians**.
To set up a trial in the United States, please email **sales@businessexpertpress.com**.

www.ingramcontent.com/pod-product-compliance
Lightning Source LLC
Chambersburg PA
CBHW061324220326
41599CB00026B/5017